From Leatherneck *to* Roman Collar

The Life and Times of
Rev. Col. Timothy Mannix Gahan, USMC (Ret.)

Colleen Gahan McFall

Order this book online at www.trafford.com
or email orders@trafford.com

Most Trafford titles are also available at major online book retailers.

Print information available on the last page.

ISBN: 978-1-6987-1075-4 (sc)
ISBN: 978-1-6987-1073-0 (hc)
ISBN: 978-1-6987-1074-7 (e)

Library of Congress Control Number: 2022900391

Trafford rev. 01/17/2022

 www.trafford.com
North America & international
toll-free: 844-688-6899 (USA & Canada)
fax: 812 355 4082

To God, faith, family, and country

The Man in the Arena

It is not the critic who counts; not the man who points out how the strong man stumbles, or where the doer of deeds could have done them better. The credit belongs to the man who is actually in the arena, whose face is marred by dust and sweat and blood; who strives valiantly; who errs, who comes short again and again, because there is no effort without error and shortcoming; but who does actually strive to do the deeds; who knows great enthusiasms, the great devotions; who spends himself in a worthy cause; who at the best knows in the end the triumph of high achievement, and who at the worst, if he fails, at least fails while daring greatly, so that his place shall never be with those cold and timid souls who neither know victory nor defeat.

Theodore Roosevelt
April 1910

Contents

Foreword

By Colleen Gahan McFall

> *"All the world is a stage, and all the men and women merely players: they have their exits and their entrances; and one man in his time plays many parts..."*

As You Like It, Wm. Shakespeare

For decades, I have watched my brother grapple with some extraordinary situations in life. Few people today have the faith, fortitude, and love of country shown in his remarkable journey. I wrote this book to share the story of his life and to inspire others.

We were raised as "army brats," moving when and where the army stationed our dad. After a short stint in college on an athletic scholarship, Tim joined the Marine Corps at age twenty, and served in Vietnam in 1966–1967. There were times in Vietnam that were high adventure; February 28, 1967, was one of those times. I was a sophomore in high school, and distinctly remember our family receiving a letter from Tim. He described one evening near Cam

Lo in Quang Tri Province, where a Marine infantry company was surrounded. The company was under heavy enemy fire and suffered numerous casualties. The unit radioed for an emergency resupply of water and ammunition. At that time Tim served as machine gunner on a CH-46A (Sea Knight) helicopter. His helicopter was assigned the mission to deliver the supplies into the "hot zone." A seasoned pilot hovered the helicopter above the position while under heavy fire and dropped the critical supplies. The pilot nursed the bullet-riddled aircraft back to the Marine base at Dong Ha. His report simply stated, "The bird sustained multiple hits." Later my brother learned that among the surrounded Marines that harrowing night was his eighteen-year-old friend LCpl Jose Holguin, who was killed in action. After Vietnam, and following graduation from North Texas State University and Officer Candidate School, Tim was commissioned and continued to serve for another quarter century, retiring at the rank of colonel.

Throughout his life, faith played a vital role. It began in our household growing up. We were imbued with a great love of the Catholic Church, and came to understand that many had suffered for the one true faith. He came home from Vietnam and married a beautiful young woman, Trisha. She was later diagnosed with multiple sclerosis and died at only thirty-five years of age. He experienced firsthand God's mercy and the consoling presence of the Blessed Virgin Mary during the difficult years caring for his ailing wife and raising two children while serving in the Corps, including many deployments. Following retirement, he became the business manager for the Priestly Fraternity of St. Peter, a community of Catholic priests, and then later the business administrator for J.E. Wilson Advisors, LCC, a small financial planning firm.

But life takes many twists and turns. "Mr. Mischief" growing up, Vietnam War veteran, and career Marine officer, Tim answered a calling to serve God and God's people as a priest. Following God's will, he celebrated his first Mass on the anniversary of his wife's death. This is the story of my brother Timothy Mannix Gahan's journey, *Deus Lo Vult* (God wills it).

Philosophy

By Rev. Col. Timothy M. Gahan, USMC (Ret.)

My sister, the author, asked me to write something on my philosophy. I was at best a mediocre student of the subject in seminary and so put her off for a while. In time I concluded that after all the work she put into her book, I could not refuse the modest request.

The word *philosophy* is from the Greek meaning "love of wisdom," and is defined as a science (that is, a certain and evident knowledge) acquired by natural reason, which is concerned with the highest of the ultimate cause of things (Attwater, *A Catholic Dictionary*). A short simple way to describe philosophy is a way of thinking about things that informs one's actions. It's really an approach to life.

As a Roman Catholic priest, my way of thinking about things is to always first consider *"the Supreme Being, infinitely perfect, who made all things and keeps them in existence"* (Baltimore Catechism). We can know there is a God through observation and reason (Rom 1:18–32), and we know there are Three Divine Persons—Father, Son, and Holy Spirit—in One God through what has been given to us from the prophets of old and the teaching and witness of Jesus Christ, God made man. My first principle is to emulate Jesus Christ, Second Person of the Trinity, so that I have life and have it more abundantly. In him, and in him alone, is found salvation. To be sure, my attempt to follow the Lord has not always been successful, and continues to be wanting, but that has not diminished and does not influence the intention. I take comfort in the words of St. Teresa of Calcutta, *"God does not require that we be successful, only that we be faithful."*

Over the years many have asked me about how it was a career Marine came to be ordained a priest. A vocation to the priesthood is truly a mystery but there are many things common to military life and the priesthood. The most prominent feature of both is a call to service; indeed, the military is often rightly described as "the service," and the priesthood is a vocation to serve God and his people. Both are ordered to the good of others. Both are countercultural. Both demand self-sacrifice. Both require total commitment— "all in" all the time. It's interesting that all five chaplains who have been awarded the Medal of Honor, our nation's highest award for heroism, since the Civil War were Roman Catholic priests. I was going to note that although military service and the priesthood are closely related there are some clear distinctions between the two. For example, military service ends and the priesthood is forever. But then I remembered, "Once a Marine, always a Marine!" Semper Fidelis!

I have been blessed with two vocations during my life, the priesthood and married life. There are distinct graces (gifts of God bestowed on the recipient through the merits of Jesus Christ for our salvation) conferred at ordination and in Christian marriage. These different graces enable the priest and married couples to live out their vocations as God intended. Grace is what animates each vocation and makes both really work.

In June 1966, while I was undergoing Marine Corps infantry training, Robert F. Kennedy delivered a speech in Cape Town, South Africa, in which he said, *"There is a Chinese curse which says '**May he live in interesting times.**' Like it or not, we live in interesting times. They are times of danger and uncertainty; but they are also the most creative of any time in the history of mankind."* The proverb is not Chinese and is actually of recent origin, and I think it is more a compliment than a curse. I have been fortunate to "live in interesting times." I served under a commanding general nearly four decades ago who once observed at a staff meeting, "We are victims of our experience." While true, another way to describe the notion is, "we are products of our experience." I am most thankful for the experience, or being the product, of living in interesting times indeed.

I have, or have had, many families: the large, affectionate family into which I was born; the warm, close family in which my late loving wife, may God rest her soul, was mother and I was father; the families in which I am a grandfather ("Pappy" to Bridey, Mary Pat, Milo, Finbar, Conan, and Betsy); my brothers in the priesthood; the Marine Corps family; a brother in fraternal organizations; and the "father" of the family of the souls that were entrusted to my spiritual care. The entry for the word "love" in the Glossary of the Catechism of the Catholic Church reads, "See Charity." The hallmark of a good family is the genuine charity that the members of the family show one another. The greater the charity for one another, the stronger the family. I have been much loved.

I believe God puts people in our lives for a reason. They nurture us, they form us, they protect us, they teach us, they encourage us, they challenge and discipline us, they lead and follow us, they lift us up, they mentor us, they celebrate and cry with us, and sometimes even die for us. On occasion they disappoint us, sometimes take advantage of us and even betray us; and often we fail them, sometimes badly so. All of them are important to the human experience. I am most grateful for those God put in my life. I considered identifying some people by name that had a memorable positive impact on me but thought the better of it for two reasons: they might not want to be highlighted, and because I would likely overlook and thereby disappoint some of the many that should be favorably mentioned. May God bless them all.

I believe we have been made for a particular purpose, that we have been given a mission from God. In describing his own life, St. John Henry Cardinal Newman put it this way: *"God has created me to do Him some definite service; He has committed some work* to me, which He has not committed to another . . . I am a link in a chain, a bond of connection between persons. He has not created me for naught. I shall do good; I shall do His work. Whatever, wherever I am, I can never be thrown away. If I am in sickness, my sickness may serve Him; in perplexity, my perplexity may serve Him; if I am in sorrow, my sorrow may serve Him. He does nothing in vain. He knows what He is about. He may take away my friends. He may throw me among strangers. He may make me feel desolate, make my spirit sink, hide my future from me—still He knows what He is about." Cardinal Newman was right; we were created to do God some definite service. The challenge for each of us, all of us, is first to discover our particular mission, and then to complete it with faithfulness. If we do, then we will be living our baptismal promise and someday hear the Father say of us what he said of his divine only begotten son at his baptism by John in the Jordan: "with you I am well pleased."

Chapter One

1967: A Memorable Year

8 March 1967
Marble Mountain Air Facility (MMAF)
Quang Nam Province, Republic of Vietnam

These last three weeks have been but a massive blur to me. I can't seem to place events in any chronological order. During the last month I had my baptism by fire; specifically been a witness and participant of this war at its grassroots. I've eaten countless boxes of C-Rations, lived in filth, had little sleep, been unbearably cold, and made probably the most lasting memories of my life. I have been mortared on, sniped at, along with receiving automatic weapons fire of assorted caliber. While at Dong Ha the other week, the other crew member on the helicopter in which I served as a gunner was hit in the foot and medevaced. The "bird" sustained multiple hits and still we flew. Names with an exotic ring—Khe Sanh, Quang Tri, Nui Loc Son, Phu Bai, Cam Lo, Hue, along with "the Rockpile," Hill 400, "Payable" and "Hill 65" are nothing more than locales at which the Cong and the "Kid" have squared off.

These lines were written by my brother Tim in a letter to our family in El Paso, Texas. When he read them more than a half century later, he was surprised our mother had kept the letter. Tim served periodically as an aerial gunner with the Marine Medium Helicopter Squadron 265 (HMM-265). The letter describes a short, noteworthy period of his thirteen-month tour of duty.

Forty-six years later, May 2013
Charleston, South Carolina

One hundred twenty people, including Vietnam veterans and their spouses, children, and grandchildren, came together at St. Mary of the Annunciation Catholic Church, the oldest Catholic church in the Carolinas and Georgia. Offering the Mass was Fr. Timothy M. Gahan, who was Lance Corporal Gahan, USMC in 1967. As the names of the twenty-nine Marines of HMM-265 who were killed in action were read, a ship's bell rang. As the bell echoed in the church, the Marine veterans remembered their fallen comrades. At the end of the Mass, Fr. Gahan walked down the aisle singing "The Marines' Hymn." Capt. Gerald Lear, a Marine Corps veteran who was in the congregation, remembered, "I was very impressed that the Roman Catholic priest knew not only the first verse, which we all know, gets to the second verse and was singing it, then the third verse, which I didn't even know there was one. I thought, 'Wow, that's pretty cool. Who is this priest?'"

At the banquet that evening, a friend of Captain Lear's said to him, "The priest wants to see you." Lear remembered, "Well, the only time the priest wanted to see me at Catholic school was when I did something bad. So, I thought, oh gee, what is that all about? So, I go and find him and . . . he says, 'Do you remember me?' And I said, 'Father, you are going to have to refresh my recollection. I'm afraid that I can't say I do.' He says, 'Do you remember a mission you flew on February 28, 1967?' I go whoa . . . it rings no immediate bells. And I say, 'Father, no, tell me why are we having this conversation?' And he said, 'Well, there was a Marine Corps company and they were out on the Demilitarized Zone (DMZ). They were surrounded by a North Vietnamese Army regiment and they needed ammunition and water.'"

Captain Lear then recalled the mission. A call for an emergency resupply had been received from the company near Cam Lo. Lear explained that if Marines call for ammo and water, it's serious. It is a mission that must be flown. At that time, they were at the Marine Corps base at Dong Ha, which was only ten kilometers south of the DMZ, and there were very few planes. Lear describes the base as "basically just a grass pad." At about five o'clock in the evening, as it was getting dark, the Marine Corps major operating the base told Lear that he would be the one to bring the supplies to the Marines in the "hot zone." The gunnery sergeant in charge of the logistics unit suggested that they construct a tall pallet to carry the supplies to the field. According to Lear, it was "just like you see when they deliver groceries to a grocery store." The gunnery sergeant said that they could transport the water in jerry cans—"like you see on the sides of Jeeps," Lear explained—and put the ammunition in boxes. The plan was that they would pile it all on the pallet, load the pallet on the ramp of the helicopter, fly it into the zone, and then drop it on the ground near the Marines. It wouldn't matter if the ammunition boxes broke, because the Marines would want to get to it right away, and the water would be delivered safely in the cans.

"I didn't know it at the time," Lear said, as he tells me the story forty-six years later, "but it was my most memorable mission." Lear's aircraft had a pilot, copilot, and two gunners. Lear was the pilot, Gahan was one of the gunners, and the other gunner and crew chief was Cpl. Joseph Pendergrass from Elk Valley, Tennessee. Lear explained the mission to his crew: they would strap the pallet to the ramp, and the two crewmen would strap themselves to the deck of the aircraft. Lear told them he would be going into the zone "hot," which meant he would be going in very fast. Once he knew where he would be dropping the supplies, he explained, he would put the aircraft up on its "hind legs" and order the crew to cut the strap, allowing the pallet to fall to the ground. Another aircraft would follow them and would go get them if they were shot down. Lear told his crew, "Now, this is going to be a hot zone and a lot of things could happen, and none of them are good." He ordered the gunners to fire when they were fired upon. "We are going to get shot," Lear informed them. Gahan later commented, "I thought it was going to be ugly. He certainly had my attention!" He described Lear's briefing as something out of the movies, only this time it was real.

The crew began its mission by flying along the DMZ. By this time, the sun had long set and it was getting hard to see. Lear called the unit they were to assist and spoke to their ground air officer about where to make the drop. "I called the frequency and identified myself and let them know that we had ammo and water. He replied that they were under heavy fire, but look for the smoke coming from a burning tank. So I ask him, 'Whose tank is it?' and he replies, 'Ours.'" Everyone on board heard this news. To his right, Lear could see the smoke coming from the burning tank, which had been hit by antitank fire. "OK, I am going to set it right next to the tank," Lear said. He quickly brought the aircraft directly toward the burning tank.

Lear described the scene: "We went in hot, and as we were going in, I could see the outline of the tank and the smoke coming up. I figured I was going to drop this pallet about twenty yards away from the tank that had already exploded. That way they could use the tank as cover to get to the ammo and water. We went in hot and hard and I pulled it up on its nose, and the minute I got it up on point, I yelled in the intercom, 'All right, cut it!' Corporal Pendergrass pulled his knife, cut it loose, and I could feel the load go. Of course, we were taking fire and you could hear the bullets pinging into the bottom of the aircraft because they make a sound like sleet or ice crystals hitting the roof. *Ping, ping-ping-ping* . . . I knew we were taking fire, because my copilot said, 'We're getting shot at!' And I said, 'Yeah, we're getting hit too!'"

After releasing the supplies, Lear put the plane in a nose-down position to gain air speed. Lear recalls, "This is always interesting because you can see right down to the ground and can see tracers coming up." At that moment, Lear heard Gahan on the radio: "Corporal Pendergrass has been hit!" Pendergrass had been shot in the right lower leg and left foot. Both gunners were strapped in

4

so that they would not fall out. Gahan was able to move around and went to help Pendergrass, but Lear remembers that Pendergrass yelled, "Get back on the gun!" Lear could then hear both .50-caliber machine guns firing. Pendergrass had managed to pull himself up and resume shooting. Lear explains, "I felt better since we were shooting back. I wheeled the aircraft around, and luckily we got out of there with a bunch of holes. Flying back all sorts of aircraft emergency lights were lit, and we were leaking hydraulic fluid. It would not be able to fly again for a couple of months, but we all got out of there in one piece except Corporal Pendergrass, who had a round in his leg and foot. If the airplane was still flying, I was flying it out. Instruments can say you're done, but I keep going if possible. I was getting it out of there."

Lance Corporal Gahan remembers the night vividly: "I remember the captain said to buckle up, that this mission could get exciting. However, there was never any question of us flying in." As Lear stated, "Marines take care of Marines. We will get there and get this done." Lance Corporal Gahan remembers, "When they opened up on us, I thought we may not get out of here." Captain Lear remembers, "There was a first aid station at Dong Ha, and we land directly at the first aid station. The corpsmen came aboard the aircraft and tried to take off Pendergrass. He didn't want to leave the airplane because he thought I was going to fly back. I had to order him off the aircraft; because he was a Marine, he wasn't going to quit. They take him off the airplane and leave Lance Corporal Gahan. I knew that my time in it was done, and the next morning we had another airplane. I go back and Lance Corporal Gahan was to stay with the original helicopter. Off I go, and then at that point I never see Lance Corporal Gahan again."

The next morning, March 1, Lear flew back to the burned-out tank and discovered that the Marine unit had held all night. It was a quiet morning and they had taken heavy casualties. He remembers, "We go in and I remember bringing medevacs on board, about fourteen at a time. I even had one on the stretcher with his head between me and the copilot. I was talking to him as we flew back, telling him that we were getting him out of there. It was a bad, bad time. We took out a lot of wounded and dead. It had been a nasty night."

"Helicopter Evacuation of the Wounded, near Hill 400," Vietnam, Operation Prairie, October 1966 Marine Medium Helicopter Squadron 265 photograph by Larry Burrows © Larry Burrows Collection

Captain Lear never thought he would meet Lance Corporal Gahan forty-six years later at a reunion. Nor did he know that Lance Corporal Gahan became a Roman Catholic priest. In addition, Gahan did not realize at the time, but during that intense battle in which they were delivering supplies on February 28, 1967, there was a young Marine in that surrounded company fighting for his life. He and Lance Corporal Gahan left the same hometown—El Paso, Texas—on the same flight, and had been in the same boot camp platoon. That eighteen-year-old Marine was killed in action that night.

LCpl Jose Holguin was born in San Ignacio, Mexico, and raised in El Paso. He was seventeen years old when he enlisted in the Marines. On March 21, 1966, his parents, Jose Sr. and Maria Holguin, went to the El Paso airport to wish their son well as he left for Marine recruit training at the Marine Corps Recruit Depot (MCRD) San Diego, California. Other young men at the airport were being seen off by their families and friends as well. My brother, twenty-year-old Timothy Gahan, was at the airport with our mom and dad. My father was a retired army colonel, and both my parents understood what it meant to serve our country.

Tim and Jose were assigned to Platoon 280, Second Recruit Training Battalion. A bond was quickly established among the men. The drill instructors (DI) were totally committed to making Marines. They were demanding and the training was arduous, but there were lighter moments. When a recruit received a package in the mail, it had to be opened in the presence of a drill instructor. The recruits had been cautioned that snacks and candy were strictly forbidden. One day, a member of Tim's squad, recruit Pvt. Johnnie Cardwell from Oklahoma, received a package. Included in Caldwell's package was a large chocolate bar, the type that schools and organizations sell for fundraisers. The drill instructor made Cardwell take the candy bar and tape it inside the lid of his footlocker. Every now and then, the DI would check to make sure the candy bar was still there, untouched. Thereafter he was always called "Private Candyman." He, like others from the platoon, was unfortunately killed in action in Vietnam. Tim remembers Cardwell as a fine young man and a good Marine.

Marine Corps Recruit Depot (MCRD) San Diego, California, May 1966. Pvt. Timothy M. Gahan at left, Pvt. Jose Holguin Jr. in the center, and Pvt. Johnnie W. Cardwell at right. Holguin died in hostile action at Cam Lo on March 1, 1967. Cardwell was killed in action in Quang Nam Province on December 2, 1966. More than 50 percent of those who served with the 1st Battalion, 1st Marines—Cardwell's unit—in Vietnam were either killed or wounded.

At that time recruit training had been compressed from thirteen to eight weeks. It included close-order drill, hand-to-hand combat training, rifle marksmanship, weapons systems training, weekly parade, and inspections. Following graduation, the new Marine would go to nearby Camp Pendleton for infantry training, which had been compressed from eight to four weeks. The training was accelerated to meet the rapidly expanding requirement for troops in Vietnam. After finishing infantry training, my brother was surprised to learn that he would be assigned to a four-week course conducted from 8:00 p.m. to 4:00 a.m., Monday through Saturday, for training in administrative duties at another location on Camp Pendleton. He had expected to receive specialized infantry training, such as machine gunner, anti-tank assaultman, mortarman, or rifleman, like most of his newly minted brother Marines. It was in infantry training where then Private Holguin and Private First Class Gahan split up.

As replacements to units in Vietnam a few months later, Private Holguin was assigned to Co L, 3rd Battalion, 4th Marines, 3rd Marine Division, and my brother to Marine Medium Helicopter Squadron 265, Marine Aircraft Group 16, 1st Marine Aircraft Wing. Both units operated mostly in the provinces in the northern part of the Republic of Vietnam.

Later, Tim learned that Lance Corporal Holguin died as the result of a gunshot wound to his chest from enemy fire during that engagement near Cam Lo, where Gahan's helicopter was delivering ammunition and water to the troops. When our parents read the newspaper announcement of Lance Corporal Holguin's funeral, they immediately made plans to attend. Tim was still serving in Vietnam, and they felt a close connection with the Holguin family. Despite the differences in background, they had much in common, especially love of their children and country.

Chapter Two

The Early Years—Lots of Places

"Quick, call a priest to administer the sacrament of Extreme Unction!" the nurse exclaimed. Timothy Mannix Gahan caused quite a ruckus from the day he was born. Our mother was hemorrhaging at home when the ambulance arrived, and they rushed her to the hospital. Her heart rate was rapid and thready, and her blood pressure was barely detectable. The last rites were administered. An emergency cesarean section was performed to save his mother's life. Tim was born on May 23, 1945, at Lawrence Memorial Hospital in Medford, Massachusetts. In the lobby of the hospital was a plaque honoring his grandfather, Dr. Patrick Francis Gahan, who practiced at the hospital in the late nineteenth and early twentieth century. In 1945, cesarean sections were a major surgery and only performed when necessary due to a patient's poor outlook for survival. Our father was a career army officer, and our mother, a former grammar school teacher, was a homemaker. At the time of Tim's birth, our parents had two daughters, Sheila and Maura, ages four and three years old; and a son, Teddy, a few days short of one year old. Another brother, Patrick, tragically died of pneumonia at three months old. At this time (World War II), our dad was serving

9

overseas in the Pacific Theater. Due to mother and baby's delicate health, our father was not notified of his birth until several days later. When Dad returned to the States from his deployment, Timmy was the same age that Teddy was when he departed.

Following World War II, the family moved to Maxwell Field, Montgomery, Alabama, where our father attended the first class of the Air War College. While there, my sister Heidi was born, in March 1947. Upon completion of the Air War College, Dad received orders to Germany as chemical officer of headquarters, US Air Forces, in Europe.

Dad went ahead of the family to Germany because a child had to be six months old to travel on the ship, and our sister Heidi was not yet old enough. The family sailed on the troop transport ship USNS *General Simon B. Buckner*. The *Buckner*, along with ships named *Patch, Rose,* and *Darby*, sailed from New York City to Bremerhaven in 1947 with dependents (wives and children) under the Army Transport Service. On its return to New York City, it carried servicemen returning from Europe. Interestingly, Tim also sailed on the *Buckner* as a Marine to Vietnam almost twenty years later.

In October of 1947, the family processed through Fort Hamilton in Brooklyn, New York, for medical exams and to complete several administrative tasks. On the day we were to depart, my mother exclaimed, "Where's Timmy?" Everyone was scrambling, looking for two-year-old Timmy. No one knew where he was! He was missing quite some time when he was finally found at a police station, eating an ice cream cone. I think that is how he got his nickname "Mr. Mischief." Finally, the family boarded the *Buckner* for a fourteen-day voyage headed for high adventure in Germany. My mother traveled with five children, ages six months to seven years old.

On the way, the ship encountered strong winds and heavy seas, and many onboard got seasick. The older children could watch movies. They sat on folding chairs that would slide from side to side whenever there were rough seas. The children thought it was great fun! There were numerous lifeboat drills. Mom recounted that it was quite an ordeal getting life jackets on five children and getting us to the abandon ship area during the drills! At the end of the two weeks at sea, the family reached Bremerhaven, West Germany. The family then boarded the train to Wiesbaden.

The family stayed in the Hotel Rose in Wiesbaden for several months, waiting for a house to be requisitioned. The German-French Ceasefire Commission used the Hotel Rose from 1945 to 1948. Our family had two suites of rooms. My oldest sister, Sheila, remembered, "It was said that our parents' suite was once occupied by Hitler. I remember as a seven-year-old, looking at the opulent rooms with gold wallpaper and cream furniture with silk upholstery." After several months, the family moved into a house on Parkstrasse. My sister Heidi's given name is Gail. However, the German domestic help confused the word "girl" with Gail, so they nicknamed her Heidi and she has been Heidi ever since. My brother Michael was born in September 1948 in Wiesbaden.

Gahan children at the Rose Hotel in postwar Wiesbaden, Germany, in 1947. Left to right, Sheila, Tim, Heidi, Maura, and Ted.

During this time, immediately post war, there was evidence that Germany had suffered greatly. There was rubble in the streets and many things could be bought on the black market for cigarettes or coffee. While living there, my family saw people going through our garbage can, taking anything edible, including potato peelings. My sister Maura states, "I remember Germans picking dandelions from our yard to make dandelion soup. Clothes were in short supply. Our mother had three blouses made of parachute material. The children relied on clothes made when scarce material was available. Our dad traced our feet on paper and sent the outlines to Sears for shoes."

In 1949, the family moved to Rottach-Ergen, Bavaria, near the Austrian border. It was a picturesque place where we lived in a lovely Bavarian-style house. We were told that it had been the summer home of Reichsmarschall Hermann Göring, who commanded the Luftwaffe, and was one of the most powerful figures in the Nazi Party. It was not far from Hitler's former mountain residence known as the "Eagle's Nest." After a few months, we moved to Bad Tolz to be closer to where dad was assigned as the chemical officer, 1st Infantry Division, "The Big Red One," a very distinguished unit. Only a few years earlier, an SS officer candidate school was in Bad Tolz. Our house had hand-carved crown molding, which included eagles and swastikas. My older sisters remember lots of beautifully carved woodwork, including a large carved totem pole-like structure that was at the base of the hand-carved banister.

On the left, Timmy was running to greet our parents when he slipped and fell. They were coming home with a camera-toting friend, who captured the moment perfectly. The picture, taken outside our house in Wiesbaden in 1948, shows his exuberant personality. On the right, the Gahan family home in Rottach-Ergin, Bavaria, in 1949.

Besides having brothers and sisters to play with, three-year-old Timmy had a German friend named Horst. "Horsty" only spoke German and Timmy only spoke English, yet they were great friends. My sisters remember Timmy and Horsty would say, *"Bitte, bitte, bonbon,"* which means "Please, please, candy." Timmy would charge candy to lend his bicycle to others. He was quite the young entrepreneur!

Our family returned to the States in August 1950 aboard the USS *General R.E. Callan.* This time it was only a ten-day crossing. Upon returning to the US, the children saw antennas on top of houses and assumed it was for televisions, which had been introduced while we were living in Germany. The family stayed in a hotel that had a TV in the room, which cost twenty-five cents an hour. The children were ready the next morning with quarters in hand to watch TV, only to discover that programming didn't start until 9:00 a.m. My sister Maura remembers, "We didn't care; we just sat there and watched the test pattern!" Dad's new assignment was as an instructor at the Chemical Corps School at Army Chemical Center, Edgewood, Maryland.

In the spring of 1951, we moved to Fort McClellan, Anniston, Alabama. The family had just finished hanging the last curtain and arranging paintings on the wall when the phone rang. My sisters remembered saying that it would be funny if it was dad saying we were moving again . . . and it was! Dad had been selected to attend the Army War College at Carlisle Barracks in Carlisle, Pennsylvania.

The few months we lived at Fort McClellan were memorable. Our quarters were next to the Officers' Mess, and the family made good use of the club's swimming pool. It was in Anniston that Timmy made his First Holy Communion. A small group of visiting nuns held a summer vacation Bible school. Teddy and Timmy were in the same class, and the nuns said, "Well, Timmy knows enough and we need another boy to make the lines just right." His First Holy Communion was a foreshadowing of Fr. Gahan offering Mass nearly six decades later.

First Holy Communion, Anniston, Alabama, spring 1951
Ted on left, Tim on right

During August 1951, the family relocated to Carlisle, Pennsylvania. I was born there and have a lovely sterling silver engraved baby cup presented to my dad from his War College classmates. Today there is a long line of bronze plaques displayed on the outer wall of Root Hall that lists alumni of the college, such as Eisenhower and Patton, and includes Col. Theodore P. Gahan among the class of 1952, the first class to graduate from the Army War College at its present location. Timmy attended first grade at St. Patrick School in Carlisle. My parents were firm believers in Catholic education and sent us to Catholic schools when feasible. There was a public school on the next block to our home, but they opted to send the four school-aged children to St. Patrick School. Our mother was the product of sixteen years of Catholic education, from first grade through college.

Following the War College, we moved to Edgewood Arsenal, Maryland, where Dad was stationed at nearby Aberdeen Proving Ground. We had quarters along the post golf course. In the second grade, Timmy attended a public school. Third grade was at St. Stephen School in 1953–54, in nearby Bradshaw. Sr. Couer de

Marie (French for "Heart of Mary") of the Sisters of St. Francis of Philadelphia was the teacher. The classes were large and the school was out in the country. My brothers Teddy and Timmy were always in the same class growing up. That worked out well for them as they developed a lifelong closeness. As Timmy has stated, "We were always together, in school, shared a bedroom, and I had a ready playmate." God gives everyone their own dignity and personality; Timmy was always impetuous, rambunctious, and talkative, while Teddy was quiet, calm, and introspective.

My sister Madonna was born at Aberdeen Proving Ground on December 16, 1954. She was due on the Feast of the Immaculate Conception on December 8; hence, she was named Madonna after the Blessed Mother. December of 1954 was a busy month, for not only was Madonna born but we also moved to Fort Jay, Governors Island, New York, when our dad was assigned as the chemical officer, First US Army. Dad brought us to our new home while my mother and sister were still in the hospital in Maryland. My mother had a cesarean section birth with Madonna, so she remained in the hospital for a week. Later my dad drove back and picked up mother and baby using our Pontiac station wagon as an ambulance. What a celebration it was when Madonna and Mom came home! It was Christmas Eve, so we had the tree decorated and there was such excitement for all to be together again. Love was all around us!

Imagine living a seven-minute ferry ride from Manhattan, New York, on an island where you could look out and almost touch the Statue of Liberty. It was an idyllic environment for kids growing up, and we lived there longer than anywhere else. When we were children, it provided us with the safety and camaraderie of a small army community.

Governors Island is 172 acres, and just 800 yards from the southern tip of Manhattan and 400 yards from Brooklyn by the Buttermilk Channel. It is rich in history as a military base for over two centuries, from the Revolutionary War until 1996. In 1524, Giovanni de Verrazzano was the first European to discover the island. At the time, the indigenous natives, the Lenape, called the island "Nut Island." The first European settlers were Dutch, and in 1624 named the island Noten Eylandt. In 1668, the British renamed Nutten Island "Governors Island" for the exclusive use of colonial governors. The island was occupied by British troops during the American Revolutionary War. After the Revolutionary War, Governors Island was transferred from the Crown to the State of New York. Fort Jay was built on the island in 1794, and Castle Williams, a circular battery, was built in 1807. During the Civil War, the island was used to muster soldiers, and Castle Williams held Confederate prisoners. The island underwent an expansion in 1912 using rocks and dirt from the excavation of the Lexington Avenue subway line and dredge from New York Harbor. The island was an army post and a quiet neighborhood for military families until November 1964. In 1966, the island was transferred to the United States Coast Guard. The Coast Guard closed its military station on Governors Island in 1995. The City of New York is now responsible for Governors Island, and charged with the operation, planning, and redevelopment of the island. The National Park Service administers the Governors Island National Monument, including Fort Jay and Castle Williams.

How did we get around the island in the mid-1950s? Well, most times we simply walked or took a bicycle since most places, such as church and school, were close by. There was also a military bus that was available for longer trips. During the six years we lived on the island, when we needed to use an automobile for off-island travel, we used our big gray Pontiac station wagon. Small ones would squeeze into the front seat between our parents, and the older ones would fill in the back seats. The youngest would ride on a tiny stool that was placed on the step just inside the side door. No seatbelts then!

When we moved to Governors Island in December 1954, Tim was in the fourth grade. We went to Post School Governors Island New York (PS 26 Manhattan), which was staffed by New York City public school teachers. It was a small school with one class of twenty to twenty-five pupils for each grade. Because of its close proximity to New York City, the school provided many educational and interesting field trips. We went to zoos, numerous museums, historic sights, and even the headquarters of the United Nations.

The school had a safety patrol, which was staffed by seventh- and eighth-grade boys. Ted and Tim were both members, and Ted was the captain. They wore big white plastic belts with badges and were stationed around the school to assist with the flow of students and traffic. They were dismissed from class early before school let out for lunch. There was not much traffic, and it was really a big deal if they had to stop a car for student crossing.

We lived on the island at Nolan Park and came home from school for lunch every day since the school was only about 150 yards from the house. We all came through the back door, and there were always sandwiches covered with a damp tea towel to keep them from drying out. Tim particularly loved the sandwiches and would praise our mother, "Mom, you make the best sandwiches!" Many times, we would have tomato soup along with the sandwiches. Yummy . . . sandwiches, soup, and a large glass of milk. We had a second refrigerator just to store our milk. We were the only family on the island who was allowed to bring the heavy wooden milk crates home from the commissary due to our large family size. My mother drove to the loading dock at the commissary to pick up seventy quarts of milk a week. Our father insisted on milk with every meal.

Children's activities today are very structured, but most of our activities on the island were organized by ourselves. We had sports teams, armies of boys from the different housing areas to play war, and even go-cart races.

Our childhood home was a happy, busy one, with many ongoing shenanigans expected in a family with eight children. My sister Madonna remembers when she was about three or four, sitting with the family around the dining table just before Christmas. Timmy excused himself and went upstairs. He proceeded to open a window and suspend a Santa Claus-costumed teddy bear, complete with bells, down to the level of the window in the dining room. He swung the teddy bear back and forth while the older Gahan children yelled, "Look, Madonna, there's Santa Claus! Hear the jingle bells of his sleigh!" Well, that cinched it for her—Santa Claus was real.

My brother Ted is on the right and Tim on the left as altar boys on Governors Island. I am in the front. My brother Michael is on the far right and a neighborhood friend is on the far left.

The Gahan brothers—Teddy, Timmy, and Mikey—were always wrestling with each other. Teddy and Timmy would have the younger Gahan sisters stand with their arms at their sides, elbows bent. Then the boys would cup our elbows and raise us high, touching our heads to the ceiling, or at least close to it. Not only did they do this to the girls but to our mom as well. All would squeal with delight, although I think mom's squeal might have been more from fright.

Our evening meal was a bonding time. Good manners were stressed and proper etiquette observed. Everyone was expected to participate in dinner conversation. Sometimes, however, this routine was disrupted. One such occasion was especially memorable. My brothers sat across from each other, Ted at my father's right and Tim at his left. During dessert, Ted said something to Tim that upset him. Tim retaliated with the only weapon at hand. He picked up a scoop of ice cream and flung it at Ted. With the same accuracy shown by David with Goliath, the glob of ice cream splattered Ted squarely in the chest. Tim instantly knew he was in hot water, so immediately bolted from the table. As he was running away, he could hear laughter coming from the dining room. The rest of us watched as Ted scrapped the ice cream off his shirt and began eating it! After that, things simmered down, but Tim was not to be found for quite a while.

The island had a sixteen-lane bowling alley that employed pin boys, including my brothers. The cost for a game was a quarter, half of which was paid to the pin boys. As Tim recalls, "You could earn what seemed like a fortune, especially if you worked two lanes at a time! We would jump in the pit and pick up the downed pins. Then we would put them in a machine above and pull a rope to set the pins. When collecting the pins, you would have to be very careful. Sometimes people would try to bowl, forgetting you were there. I was not allowed to set pins during the school week, only Friday night, Saturday, and sometimes Sunday afternoon." The island commissary allowed boys to bag groceries. Timmy and Teddy worked as "baggers." There were two bag boys for each checkout aisle, who worked for tips only, about a nickel per bag. Working at the commissary, baggers learned about people and life.

In the spring, Little League came to the island, and almost every boy participated in it. During the fifth grade season, Timmy was the All-Star second baseman. The following year, he was an All-Star pitcher and utility outfielder. He received a trophy for Most Valuable Player of the 1956 Eagles team.

There was a small indoor shooting range on the island, and a marksmanship program for boys and girls. Youngsters met on Saturdays and fired .22 caliber rifles. My brothers, Teddy and Timmy, belonged to Troop 100 Manhattan, a quite active Boy Scout troop. They had their own scout lodge. Scouts were issued uniforms and camping equipment, mostly World War II army surplus— knapsacks, mess kits, axes, etc. By the end of grammar school, both boys earned the rank of Star Scout.

In the summer of 1958, the scouts of Troop 100 had an incredible opportunity to go to the Caribbean. Arrangements were made for the boys to travel from New York City to the naval station at Guantanamo Bay, Cuba, and then to San Juan, Puerto Rico, aboard the troop transport USS *General George M. Randall*. On arrival at Guantanamo Bay, they set up at a campsite on a beautiful bluff overlooking the small bay at Holiday Beach. Plenty of activities were planned and Cuban Boy Scouts joined in some of them. Tim still has a hand-carved wooden letter opener that he bought in Cuba as a present for our parents. Shortly before the scouts arrived in Cuba, a bus with sailors and Marines was hijacked near the town of Guantanamo. There was increased tension, and no one was allowed to leave the base.

One especially memorable activity was firing weapons supervised by Marines from the Marine barracks. Tim recalls, "The Browning automatic rifles were heavy, and I remember it ejected hot brass casings. When I went to get up from the firing position, my forearm rolled over on a piece of hot brass. It left a souvenir mark from Cuba that I wore proudly for several months." Interestingly, just a few months after the scout trip, Elvis Presley was photographed walking up the gangway of the USS *Randall* to set sail to serve in the 3rd Armored Division in West Germany.

Always the hard worker, during grades five to eight, Tim delivered the evening and Saturday morning newspapers for the entire island. The two newspapers he delivered were the *New York Journal American* and the *New York World-Telegram and Sun*. Neither is in business today. Tim would ride his bike to the ferry dock and travel to Manhattan to pick up a bundle of each newspaper. He always hoped that the newspapers would be there so he could just jump right back on the ferry. On the ride back, he would open up the bundle and fold up the papers and put them into a canvas delivery sack with a shoulder strap. Then he would get on his bike with all the papers rolled up to begin deliveries. Tim had all his customers' names memorized. For some deliveries he would get off the bike and run up to the door and drop the paper. For others he would throw them to hit the door. He didn't have plastic sacks to go over the newspaper like today, so in bad weather there was no throwing. If it was snowing, usually the streets were clear, but paperboys were still fighting snowdrifts and a bitter wind coming off the water. The weather could really slow him down. Sometimes

Tim's classmates would come with him and wait at the ferry station waiting room, where there was a nickel candy bar machine. Tim would get a candy bar to share. Every once in a while, he would stop at the Officers' Club, where a generous scoop of ice cream was only a nickel.

Tim's newspaper delivery boss was Harry Merski. When Tim took the paper route in fifth grade, he was taller than Harry. Harry was short, mostly bald, and wore gloves with the fingers cut out. He would meet Tim on Saturdays and pay him $5 a week to deliver about fifty papers a day. Harry ordered newspapers in groups of five. He would calculate some customers were out of town and suspend delivery of their newspaper. As an example, if Tim was to deliver thirty-two *World-Telegram* newspapers, to save money, Harry would order thirty, not thirty-five. Every now and again, Tim would not have enough papers to cover deliveries. The first time it happened, Tim told Harry that he didn't have enough papers. Harry responded, "You figure it out! You know if someone is out of town!" Tim said no, he didn't have enough papers and felt that if people are paying for their newspaper, they should get it. So Harry said, "OK, I'll tell you what, the Officers' Club has ordered two *Journal American* and two *World-Telegram* newspapers. If you are short newspapers, short the club." Later that week, Tim was short and delivered only two newspapers instead of four to the club. The next day, when Tim went to the club, the club manager asked Tim, "How many newspapers do we get?" Tim stated four newspapers but that sometimes he delivered two or three. The manager asked, "Why not four?" Tim explained, "Harry Merski told me that if I am short newspapers, to short the club because you are not home delivery." The next Saturday when Tim went to get his pay and updated customer list, Harry was waiting. Harry screamed, "What are you doing telling them about shorting the club!" After that episode, Tim never had any problems getting the correct number of newspapers. In fact, he often had extras, which he sold at the hospital.

After working with Harry for a while, Tim said, "Harry, I have to have at least $5.50 a week." Tim was getting $5 a week at the time. "Look," Tim said, "that isn't even a dollar a day." Harry yelled, but then agreed. Tim learned valuable life lessons working with Harry Merski.

Gahan family on Governor's Island, 1960. Tim is on the back row, first on the left. I am on the front row, second from the left, directly in front of my mother.

Chapter Three

Power, Burges, and Cisco

T he transition from grammar school to high school is always challenging. The change from being a proud and happy member of the senior class at one school to being numbered among the lowest and youngest members at another is a difficult one. Leaving a small, isolated coeducational school staffed by women for a large, inner-city all-boys Roman Catholic school operated by the no-nonsense Irish Christian Brothers can be shocking. The ICBs had an enviable reputation: they were scholars in religious vows who commanded great respect and demanded the best of those entrusted to their educational care. They were holy educators who booked no foolishness and got favorable results. They were tough men of strong faith, sterling role models, and had a joyful community spirit.

Tim completed grammar school on Governors Island in the spring of 1959. Since there was no high school on Governors Island, all high schoolers would take the ferry to Manhattan, Staten Island, or Brooklyn to attend school. To attend Catholic schools in the New York City area, potential students were administered a Catholic New

York City-wide entrance exam. Both brothers, Tim and Ted, were accepted to Power Memorial Academy.

Power Memorial Academy was operated from 1931 to 1984 by the Irish Christian Brothers. The school was well known and highly regarded for its athletic prowess, especially in basketball, in addition to rigorous academics. The UCLA All-American and Los Angeles Lakers superstar Kareem Abdul-Jabbar (then Lew Alcindor) played for Power Memorial Academy from 1961 to 1965. Its 1964 basketball team was named by national sports writers "the number one high school team of the century."

In the fall of 1959, every boy entering freshman year was summoned to bring a pair of sneakers and shorts, and meet at a little park in Midtown Manhattan near the Hudson River. All were timed running the half mile, and that is how the freshman cross-country team was recruited. That tryout sparked my brothers' interest in cross-country running and track. Ted became the star of the freshman cross-country team and track team. Tim also did well, and both earned varsity letters their sophomore year.

My brothers Ted (on the left) and Tim (on the right) as members of the Power Memorial Academy cross-country team. They both earned varsity letters their sophomore year.

Power Memorial Academy was academically demanding. For three years, there were few choices of courses. Not surprisingly, students were required to take four years of Latin, four years of religion, four years of math, four years of science, and seniors could take one choice of class. The faculty was predominately of Irish heritage, and all were strict disciplinarians. Discipline was usually enforced on the spot with a strap. In the classroom, all stood when a teacher entered, and then he led a prayer. On occasion students remained standing and the teacher might ask something like third person, plural imperfect of a Latin verb or a translation of a noun. If one answered correctly, he was allowed to sit down. If not, the student remained standing and had to put out his hand for the teacher to smack it with a strap.

The school was in a high-rise building at the corner of Sixty-First Street and Amsterdam Avenue in Manhattan. Students were not allowed to use the elevators. The only exception was when my brother Ted was recovering from mononucleosis. If a young man was assigned detention, he served it that day. There were no excuses accepted to delay it. If you missed it, then you would have to attend two consecutive detentions. Tim remembers, "We sat side to side on backless benches with our hands on our knees, and sat looking at the clock on the wall. No talking, no flinching. If you did, you earned another detention. They didn't care if you had a dentist or doctor appointment. I believe if you had died, they would have propped your body up in detention." Tim stated, "Yes, it was unpleasant, but I only was subjected to it a few times."

The Irish Christian Brothers, like so many religious communities after the Second Vatican Council, declined precipitously in vocations. They consolidated with other orders, and are now the Congregation of Christian Brothers. Besides the athletics and academics, a major component of Catholic education was the strong religious foundation it provided. Tim recounts how grateful he was to our parents for sending their sons to the school. Brothers taught classes, and there were periodic school Masses, daily religion classes, and prayer recited throughout the day. Both boys belonged to the Sodality of the Blessed Virgin Mary, which was an organization dedicated to the Blessed Mother. Perhaps this background was important to Tim's discernment to the priesthood many years later.

To get to school, the boys took the ferry to Manhattan every day from Governors Island to the South Ferry Terminal, then took the subway to Fifty-Ninth Street and walked to the school at Amsterdam and Sixty-First Street. The location was adjacent to what is now the Lincoln Center for the Performing Arts. Most days the boys would have cross-country or track practice after school, which was held in

Van Cortlandt Park in the Bronx, Central Park in Manhattan, or an armory. They would get home very late in the evening. At home, they would then dine late and have at least two hours of homework every night. Tim remarked, "That was quite an education. I learned a lot in those two years. It was good preparation for the Marine Corps." Much to Tim's surprise, the 1961 yearbook stated, "The class has lost its most outstanding member when Tim Gahan moved to Texas." Tim stated later, "Man, I must have been somebody!"

Our father retired in 1961, and we relocated to El Paso, Texas, in part because of the mild climate and close proximity to two major military installations, Ft. Bliss and William Beaumont Army General Hospital. My father joined the faculty at Burges High School, the same school where my brothers enrolled, where he taught chemistry, physics, and later, history. Burges was a big change from Power Memorial. It was secular, coed, and the academics, while very good, were not as rigorous. The high school was within easy walking distance of our home.

Tim came in as a junior and joined the cross-country team. For training, the coach would periodically drive the team well out into the desert (remember, this is El Paso, with lots of desert), drop them off miles away, and have them run back to the school. The team was competitive, trained hard, and became a group of good friends. In the spring, Tim ran the mile, finishing up as runner-up in the District Junior Varsity Championship. The following year, he moved up to varsity.

In the f all of 1962, the Burges High School cross-country team, led by captain Ted Gahan, won the District 1-AAAA (largest-size school) and state championship. It was the first state championship for the school in any sport. The following spring, Ted won the mile run in the district championship. He finished runner-up in the same event in the state championship with a school record time of 4:20 despite running with a leg injury. Tim also had a successful senior year in track and field competition.

Under the headline "Burges Wins Track Title With 1-2-3 Sweep in Mile," the lead paragraph on the front page of the Sports Section of the *El Paso Times* newspaper on Friday, April 12, 1963, read: *A 1-2-3 sweep in the mile run boosted Burges High School to the District*

1-AAAA track championship Thursday on the Mustangs' home field." The article went on to record, *"The three milers were Ted Gahan, Bob Smith and Tim Gahan, in that order. Ted Gahan and Smith grabbed an early lead and were never threatened. But Tim Gahan, Ted's brother, had to move up from the middle of the pack to finish third, overtaking Bowie's Arturo Martinez on the final turn."* The following week, the school newspaper described the race this way: *"In one of the outstanding races of the day all three Burges runners finished 1-2-3 in the mile run. Finishing first was Ted Gahan with a 4:31.1 timing followed by Bob Smith and Tim Gahan."* The article continued: *"While the crowd watched the Gahan-Smith duel, Tim Gahan, Ted's younger brother broke from the pack and steadily gained on the leaders. Coming off the final turn of the race Tim, running the best mile of his high school career, passed Tech's Augie Chavez, and Bowie's Martinez to give Burges the rare sweep of the top three places."*

Burges Takes Title

Cindermen Decisive District Champs; Break Records; Look to Regional Meet

by Marc Davidson

The Burges track team, paced by record performances by Pat Riordan, Craig Van Auken, and Gregg Marr, outscored eight other district schools to win the Mustangs' second district track championship in three years April 11, on the Burges track.

The Mustangs ran up 128 points to defeat Tech and Bel Air who scored 92 and 82 points respectively. Fourth was Ysleta with 68 points followed by Austin 61, El Paso High 47, Bowie 11, Jefferson 5 and Irvin 2.

Mile is All-Burges

In one of the outstanding races of the day all three Burges milers finished 1-2-3 in the mile run. Finishing first was Ted Gahan with a 4:31.1 timing followed by Bob Smith and Tim Gahan. Ted's time was only 2.5 seconds off the district record set in 1948. Ted and Bob alternated taking the lead every half-lap until the final lap when Ted took the lead from Bob. Ted took the victory also by outsprinting Bob in the final 220.

While the crowd watched the Gahan-Smith duel, Tim Gahan, Ted's younger brother, broke from the pack and steadily gained on the leaders. Coming off the final turn of the race Tim, running the best mile of his high school career, passed Tech's Augie Chavez and Bowie's Martinez to give Burges the rare sweep of the top three places.

Riordan Breaks Record

Pat Riordan was the first Mustang to break a record in the two day meet when he threw the discus 160' 9½".

The old record was 156' 2¾ inches set last year. Tom Hughes won second place with a throw of 154' 2" while Roger Stanberry finished fifth. Riordan and Hughes will compete in the discus competition April 20, at the Regional meet in Odessa.

Gregg Marr broke the old record in the pole vault as he leaped 12' 5¾ inches. The old mark was 12' set in 1961. After setting his record Marr missed three times at 12' 11" in an attempt to set an all-time record. Mike Boyd finished fourth in the event. Marr will also go to Odessa to compete in the pole vault and mile relay.

Fifth in Relay

Burges finished a distant fifth in the 440 relay as the Mustang anchor man, Joe Tirrell, was hobbled by a foot injury which prevented him from placing in the 100 yard dash.

The Mustangs finished first and second in the half mile as Craig Van Auken ran a blazing 1:58.1 into a strong wind to break the old district record of 1:58.7. Raul Vela nailed down the second position as he sped by Ysleta's Sosa who faltered coming off the final turn of the race. Both boys will compete in the 880 at the Regional meet.

Marr Tallies in Hurdles

Gregg Marr was credited with fourth place in the high hurdles and gathered four points toward his total of 18.

Randy Capshaw won third place in both the 100 and 220 yard dashes, narrowly missing a trip to Odessa.

Tim Hughes won first place in the shot put to give the Mustangs their only points in the event. Hughes throw was 55', one of his best of the year.

Burges won six points in the high jump as Ervie Robinson tied for third and Herb McNeely won sixth place.

The Mustang mile relay team of Stanley Woods, Tony Alexander, Gregg Marr, and Craig Van Auken finished second behind Ysleta for the first time this year but still earned a trip to the regional competition in Odessa.

Burges Holds Seven Records

Burges now owns seven out of the fourteen district records. The Mustangs hold the record in the 220, low hurdles, high hurdles, 440 relay, half mile, discus, and pole vault. No other school holds more than two records. The records in the remaining seven events are divided among five schools.

Burges, which is rapidly challenging Ysleta for the position of the perennial track power, has now finished either first or second in the district meet for the last five years.

BOB SMITH, TED GAHAN, and TIM GAHAN (left to right) stand above their respective positions in the mile run during the District 1-AAAA track meet. The unusual sweep clinched the pennant for the Mustangs.

Burges High School in April 1963 student newspaper article describing the 1-2-3 sweep in the mile run of the District 1-AAAA track championship. The three milers were Ted Gahan, Bob Smith, and Tim Gahan, to give Burges the rare sweep of the top three places.

Over a half century later, Fr. Gahan recalled the race in a homily he delivered to students at St. Joseph High School in Greenville, South Carolina:

> *The economy of our great nation is in a sorry state. Unemployment remains stubbornly high; the financial sector is under strain; and in many places the housing market is dismal. It is becoming increasingly difficult to get a good return on investment anywhere. Amidst all this, there is still one thing that guarantees a handsome return if we invest in it with discipline. That thing is Lent, and the return is superabundant joy in the celebration of the Resurrection. Simply put, the more we are committed to the Lenten practices of increased prayer, fasting, alms-giving, and the like, the greater will be our rejoicing at Easter; and the dividends will continue to be paid long after the lilies have wilted.*
>
> *In thinking of a way to express this idea of return on investment, I thought of when I was a miler on the high school track team. I was a mediocre runner during my freshman, sophomore, and junior years. Oh, I was faithful to training and enjoyed it, but I wasn't really invested in it, and did not have much success. Midway through my senior year, it occurred to me that my competitive running days were rapidly coming to a close, and I resolved to take the sport seriously. I did not want to answer the question, "How good might I have been if I really applied myself?" in later years . . . or perhaps my real motivation was that I wanted to impress my girlfriend. In any event, I sweated and strained for hours each day to become stronger and faster. I looked forward to the demanding daily workouts that left me completely exhausted. Soon it seemed I was thriving on the regimen. It was the most difficult thing I had done in my young life, yet I truly enjoyed it. In the district championship,*

the last meet of the season, we competed against more than two dozen teams; and with two events remaining, the mile and the mile relay, our team was in second place. What was to be the return on my investment? As expected, our other two milers finished first and second, but running far faster than anyone thought possible, I finished a surprisingly close third, in four minutes and thirty-six seconds. Not only had I far exceeded expectations, with the points we scored in that event, our team had won the championship. All the sacrifice was well worth the unforeseen result. So it is with Lent. The more we invest ourselves in what we do or do not do during Lent, the more we will take to it, grace building upon grace throughout these forty days. And the great benefit will be not only to us, but our team, the community of believers, as well. The whole purpose of Lent is to prepare ourselves for the championship—Easter. It is a time for serious spiritual workouts . . . a time to make ready for the passion, death, and resurrection of Christ. Will what we do be worth the effort? I assure you the return on the investment will be out of this world. Train hard. I sometimes wonder what became of that girl.

A few years later, when Tim was between college graduation and the start of Marine Corps Officer Candidates School, he returned to Burges High School and assisted coaching the track team. My younger sister Madonna, a Burges student at the time, remembers, "There was a student/faculty basketball game at Burges. Since Tim was quasi-faculty, he was on the team. He loved it. He chewed his gum furiously as he would run up and down the court, waving his arms for his teammates to throw him the ball. I don't know how many points he made, but I know I was proud to acknowledge him as my brother as classmates asked, to no one in particular, 'Who is that guy?'"

Years later, in 1971, Tim was named as that year's Outstanding Ex-Student of Burges High School. He flew in from Camp

Pendleton, California, to receive the award, and was asked to speak at the homecoming pep rally. If anyone knows how to energize a crowd, Tim does. He had the crowd on their feet, cheering wildly, especially as he concluded his speech. He paused, and looking directly at the football players, yelled, "Give them hell!" My sister Madonna, who was there, said, "Well, that word had never been intentionally used before in a school event. Needless to say, Tim (and me since I was his family) was considered 'way cool.'"

Tim had a respectable high school academic record, even making the honor roll periodically, and at the suggestion of our father, applied for admission to the newly established Texas Maritime Academy. The school was part of Texas A&M University, and most of the program was to be based in Galveston. He was pleased to be accepted to the first class. At the same time, my brother Ted had a few track scholarship offers after he finished second in the State of Texas high school championship with a time of 4:20. One very generous offer ("full ride" except a room fee for one semester) was from Cisco Junior College. Ted declined the offer, as he was discerning a vocation to the priesthood, and was going to a seminary in the fall. He let the track coach at Cisco know that he had a younger brother who ran a four-minute thirty-six second mile. So as fortune would have it, Cisco offered Tim the same scholarship, and Tim quickly accepted it.

Tim enjoyed Cisco Junior College; his time there was interesting and memorable. For example, the athletic dorm for boys, Bivins Hall, the oldest building on the campus, was quite a lively place. As Tim remembers, "You always had to be on guard because of the ongoing horseplay and pranks. Sports and enjoying college life seemed far more important to the athletes than academics. It certainly was a fun place to live."

My sister Sheila and her husband, Joe, visited Tim while he was at Cisco. She recalls, "As we parked the car in front of the athletic dorm, an armadillo ran desperately out the front door, chased by several football players in hot pursuit. I don't know if they ever caught the armadillo, but that was our introduction to his dorm. Tim showed us his room and—oh my, it was just as we expected it to be!"

The upper floor rooms of Bivins Hall housed the football players. The basketball players were assigned to the ground level on one side, and the other side were multisport athletes. There was no air-conditioning or central heat. For heat, there were gas heaters in individual rooms, with a brass tube that ran to a small stove in the middle of the room to take out the chill. On the upper floor, there was a decorative balcony that had no entrance from inside the building. When the weather was nice, some of the guys, mostly football players, decided to knock out part of the wall to get to the balcony area and drag mattresses out to lie among the chunks of mortar and broken brick. More than once, as college girls passed by the dorm, the football players threw chunks of masonry at them, causing the girls to scream and run.

The showers at Bivins Hall were a special entertainment. Residents would plug the drain with towels, and it would flood the bathroom with six to eight inches of water, making it like a swimming pool in which to splash about.

Behind Bivins Hall was a small Student Union building. There was a ping-pong table and a pool table. Snacks, ice cream, and Cisco Junior College paraphernalia, including small inexpensive rings, were sold there. One night the building was burglarized. Soon after, several boxes of melted ice cream were found behind Bivins Hall, and later some of the athletes were seen walking around with rings on sticky fingers.

One day, an elderly farmer came to the dorm recruiting help to harvest peanuts in nearby Gorman, Texas. About six to eight students, all Yankees, were eager to earn some spending money. When they returned, they looked more dead than alive. They had been bent over all day and could hardly stand. Their necks were red with sunburn, and their eyes were swollen from rubbing them with their hands covered in peanut dust. The students from northern states learned the hard way about Texas farm life.

After one semester living in Bivins Hall, Tim talked it over with our dad about moving to another dorm. The academic dorm nearby, Cluck Hall, had a two-hour quiet time in the evening for studies. It was much more conducive to studying, so Tim made the change.

The rooms and facilities in the new dormitory were in far better condition than Bivins Hall.

Living in a small Texas town exposed Tim to a different culture. For example, the food was quite different. He had never had iced tea. At home, tea was always hot. He also didn't have fried foods growing up, and was not familiar with food such as grits, black-eyed peas, or collard and mustard greens. Tim remembers, "The local fare was right tasty. I quickly grew to like country food."

The town of Cisco had an interesting history, especially during the oil boom of the 1920s and '30s. It had the first hotel by Conrad Hilton, and at one time boasted the world's largest concrete swimming pool. The enrollment of Cisco Junior College was approximately 200 students, which was smaller than the graduating class of Burges High School. Most of the students were from small towns in West and Central Texas, but there were also students from all over the country living in the Bivins Hall on athletic scholarships. There were very few Catholics, the town was in the buckle of the "Bible Belt." They had an older circuit priest from Ireland who offered Mass on Sunday. A lot of the Catholic jocks recruited by the college were from out of state. Tim was the only Texan who was Catholic. The Catholic students from the Northeast were real rascals, but always took the obligation to attend Sunday Mass seriously. Tim remembers them even taking someone's car without permission to drive to Mass.

Cisco Junior College's track was made of dirt. It was rough and not quite regulation, and would puddle badly after a rain. Tim was running the mile and two-mile, and sometimes ran the 880-yard event as well. The first year, Tim struggled when running due to a nagging knee injury. The coach sent him to a chiropractor to help. When the season was complete, Tim went to talk to the coach about continuing his scholarship. As Tim recalls, "I went to see the coach, and the coach said, 'You know, I am really sorry.' I thought, 'Oh boy, so much for my scholarship.' Then the coach continued, 'I won't be able to increase your scholarship from last year.' What!? Wonderful! I was so relieved!" Tim was able to improve his running the second year. He never won races, but scored points in most all track meets, including the Texas Junior College Track and Field Championship.

Tim running track at Cisco Junior College, May 1964

Not only did Tim run better in his second year, he improved his grades as well. He was more settled. To this day, he fondly remembers his time there. Perhaps the reason the two years at Cisco JC were so memorable is because he was young, living on his own 500 miles from home, and experiencing college life in a small West Texas town. As of this writing, Tim's (now Fr. Gahan's) bucket list includes offering Holy Mass at the small Our Lady of the Holy Rosary Catholic Church in Cisco.

In May 1965, Tim enrolled in the Marine Corps Platoon Leader Course. It consisted of two six-week training periods during college, with commissioning upon graduation. Tim completed the first summer training at the Marine Corps base in Quantico, Virginia, in July.

Following Cisco JC, Tim went on to Angelo State College (now Angelo State University), which had just changed from a two-year to a four-year college. The school was not a good fit for Tim. He recalls that he was unhappy there due to a lack of maturity. It didn't work out because he was unfocused, so he decided to enlist in the Marines. The Vietnam War was underway, and everyone knew that a healthy young man was going to serve in the military. It was just a matter of when and which branch of the armed forces. He chose the Marines based on his favorable experience in the PLC program, and he liked the idea of belonging to a unique and historic group with rich traditions. Tim states, "It was an opportunity to be a part of something larger than yourself, to pay your dues, grow up a little, develop some self-discipline, and serve our country."

Chapter Four

Camp Fatima—Summers in New Hampshire

"*Je vous salue, Marie, pleine de grâces,*" the camper recited at night in the camp cabin in the woods. Imagine being a ten-year-old and only speaking French at an English-speaking summer camp. You were French-Canadian, and your parents sent you to a Catholic camp for boys in New Hampshire. This is what many young boys attending Camp Fatima in the 1950s and 1960s experienced. Their parents wanted an English-immersion environment to practice English, and a good Catholic summer camp. Many nights, each cabin prayed the rosary together. The French-Canadian boys would say their decade in French, and the Americans would say their decade in English. As time went on in the camping season, the French Canadians learned their prayers in English, and the others learned their prayers in French. That is how my brothers learned to pray the Hail Mary in French.

Preparing for a crowning of the Blessed Virgin Mary. Tim is on the right.

One constant for the Gahan siblings was Camp Fatima for boys and Camp Bernadette for girls in New Hampshire. Tim attended as camper or staff member for at least some part of the summer from 1952 to 1965. In 1952, Timmy had just turned seven and began his first year at Camp Fatima. Most years we were all traditionally known as "seasoners," staying for two months. Timmy was assigned to a cabin with his brother Teddy and slept in the cot nearest to the counselor. My parents figured that even though they were young, they always had each other for support.

Camp Fatima was founded in 1949 by the dynamic and charismatic Fr. Richard Boner. It had about 300 boys organized in three divisions—Junior, Intermediate, and Senior—with eight to fourteen boys per cabin. Camp Fatima is located near Gilmanton Ironworks, New Hampshire, in the scenic Lakes Region. Many of the counselors were seminarians. We became acquainted with the camp through our cousins, the Walsh family. The eldest Walsh, "Corbie," attended camp that first year, and was awarded the "Model

Camper" award. He went on to become a Jesuit priest, Fr. E. Corbett Walsh, SJ.

After supper, campers were given a dime to spend at the camp canteen. That dime was rubbed between grimy fingers as campers fussed over choosing between a candy bar or ice cream for an after-dinner treat. Corbie, like the others, received his daily ten cents for the entire camp season, but he saved every dime. Not long after he returned home at the end of the camp season, he walked to the local hardware store and bought a new iron for his mother with the money he saved. All summer long he denied himself to purchase a gift for her.

There was a solid Catholic character to the camp. Each day started with Mass in the rustic chapel, followed by a reflection at the adjoining shrine. In the evenings, campers would have benediction in the camp chapel and process to the shrine for short prayers. Afterward, campers would file back to the cabins, where they would pray the rosary after turning in. Following breakfast each morning, the boys would go back to the cabins and clean their space. There was always fierce competition to be named the "Honor Cabin" after inspection.

Campers were assigned different activities throughout the day, including tennis, horseback riding, swimming instruction, baseball, basketball, archery, boxing, riflery, arts and crafts, woodworking, soccer, and boating activities such as canoeing, water skiing, and sailing. Tim especially liked sailing, canoeing, and the two free swims a day.

There were other organized activities outside of camp, such as the Mount Washington boat trip on Lake Winnipesaukee; time spent at a pioneer camp in the Waterville Valley; and mountain climbing on Bear Mountain, Mount Chocorua, Mount Osceola, and Tripyramid Mountain. Other special activities included the Camp Olympics, involving many sports events. The summer Tim turned fifteen, his final year as a camper and while a CIT (counselor in training), he was named "Best Athlete" for his performance in running and swimming competitions.

Evening activities included competitions such as "Capture the Flag" and "Where's Kelly?" The games sometimes got brutal. With

100 boys determined to win, some finished the games with bloody noses or sprains, and scratches and bruises were common. There were many trips to the infirmary after night activity.

Most Saturday nights featured hotdogs and beans around the campfire and the singing of American and French-Canadian songs. Then the campers would all head off for boxing matches at an outdoor ring. In 1952, when Tim had just turned seven, he won the fourth-place ribbon in the seven-, eight-, and nine-year-old division of approximately 100 boys. In 1954, as a nine-year-old, he won the first-place blue ribbon in that age division.

They used oversized gloves because the heavier the glove, the lighter the punch. A ring announcer introduced the competitors and also served as referee. Boxers would come out and touch gloves to begin the match. Those three or four one-minute rounds seemed to last much longer, and the whole camp would turn out to cheer on the fighters.

For many years the Camp Fatima promotional brochure featured Tim. He remembers wearing a Camp Fatima shirt, and a photographer asked to take his picture while he was eating in the mess hall. Tim states, "I remember the meal being cold cuts and potato chips, and holding a knife and fork beside the plate. I was surprised to see myself in the camp brochure, which was used for quite some time."

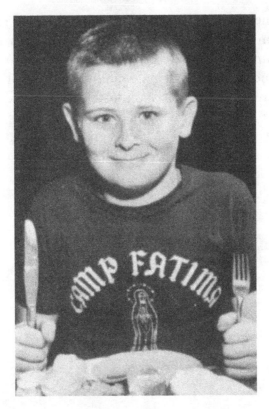

Camp Fatima brochure picture. Always ready to eat!

As the Gahan brothers got older, all were on staff at the camp. Our dad was the program director for the camp in 1961 and senior division head in 1962. My brother Teddy was also program director and head of the waterfront. Years later, our brother Michael was also senior division head one summer. Tim served as counselor, and during that time started a track and field program. He taught boys how to throw the discus and shot put, built high jump and long jump pits, organized short relay races, and trained sprinters.

Senior campers at night sometimes would listen to a radio on low volume. "Sometimes we were allowed to listen to a baseball game," Tim recalled. "There were no phones, no TV, or any electronic devices except a radio, which was great. I think it should be that way today." All the Gahan siblings were fortunate that our parents sacrificed for us to be able to attend summer camp.

Tim's time as a camper or staff member at Camp Fatima ended in 1965. Tim's son Terence maintained the family tradition of attending camp for many years, as both a camper and counselor. In fact, Terence recalls, "With the multiple moves with our family, attending Camp Fatima was one constant in my life." Many years later, in 2016, two of Tim's grandsons from Texas, Finbar and Conan, were campers there. With his grandsons in attendance, the now Fr. Timothy Gahan celebrated Mass in the same camp chapel that he attended for so many years.

Chapter Five

Vietnam

"We were rocking and shaking for two long days and nights, slammed by a typhoon in the Pacific, as we traveled from San Diego to Da Nang, Vietnam, on the USNS *General Simon B. Buckner* in September 1966. There were about 2,000 troops on the ship, mostly US Marines and a company of US Army Military Police. We were in the bottom of the ship, with bunks side by side stacked four or five high. The bunks consisted of canvas stretched over metal tube framing connected to a pole by a chain, allowing the bunks to be drawn up during the day. We used our life vests for pillows and had our sea bags/duffle bags between our legs, making it difficult to turn over. It was very close quarters, and many suffered sea sickness from the rocking ship," Tim remembered.

A year earlier, while at Cisco Junior College, Tim enrolled in the Marine Corps PLC program (Platoon Leaders Course). It was a program similar to ROTC designed for college students to be commissioned as a Marine officer after graduation. He spent six weeks in training at the USMC base at Quantico, Virginia, during the summer of 1965, then a semester at Angelo State College. He dropped out of school and enlisted in the Marines in February 1966. The Vietnam War was expanding, and the armed services were growing rapidly to meet the increased demand for personnel.

After boot camp, Tim completed infantry training where Marines were thoroughly drilled in weapons and tactics. Following a monthlong course on administrative duties and a short leave in the summer of 1966, he joined the Staging Battalion at Camp Pendleton for another month of infantry training before shipping out to Vietnam.

Private First Class Gahan on leave in El Paso during the summer of 1966, with Mom and Dad before reporting to Staging Battalion.

Tim sailed out of San Diego the day after Labor Day. It took three weeks, which included a brief refueling stop in Okinawa, to get to Da Nang. Interestingly, all Marines who were only seventeen years old debarked in Okinawa and waited until they were eighteen to continue on to Vietnam. This was the season of typhoons, and an unexpected typhoon forced the ship to change course for a few days.

Years later, Fr. Gahan remembered in a homily:

> *Our gospel reading today reminded me of when I was a young Marine embarked on a troop ship on the edge of a typhoon in the South China Sea in 1966. For two days and two nights, the ship was continuously battered by enormous waves, buffeted by howling winds, and pelted by torrential rains. It was a fearsome thing. The sea can be terrifying and unforgiving. Our gospel is not, however, a lesson in the power of nature; rather, the message is to place our trust in the Lord, especially when we find ourselves unexpectedly tossed about on the sea of life. The memory of Jesus calming the sea and saving his disciples must have had a quieting effect on his followers in the midst of the great struggles and difficulties they experienced after the Ascension. It should help us do the same. In him, and in him alone, is there freedom from fear and anxiety. Just as Jesus calmed the sea and quieted the wind when the apostles called upon him to save them, he will do the same for us if we call upon him in faith to help us, no matter how dire the situation. He wants us to wake him and say to him, "Lord, save us! We are perishing!" especially in times of severe distress. He will answer us, be with us, calm the storms of our lives, and see us safely to shore. Fair winds, following seas, and may God always keep you in his loving care.*

While on the ship, chow was served by having the men form a line that would snake all around the ship, through passageways and ladder wells. It was not unusual to wait in the chow line for an hour or longer. On the mess deck there were narrow tables about chest high with no seats. This was an efficient way to feed large numbers in a limited space. Breakfast consisted of a bowl of oatmeal and a mug of black coffee, and took only minutes to consume. That is where Tim learned to drink coffee. Many would start to line up for lunch shortly after breakfast because they knew it was going to be a long line.

PFC James Gannone from New Jersey was a brother Marine from the Staging Battalion on the ship. He wrote in his book *The Rest Is Small Potatoes*, "Traveling via troop ship isn't a Carnival Cruise to the Caribbean. Most of the time at sea on a troop ship is consumed with waiting in line for chow. The chow line for every meal wrapped around the entire deck at least twice." There is a picture in the book of James, a very colorful character, and Tim on board the *Buckner* headed to Vietnam.

Aboard the USNS *General Simon B. Buckner* with (left to right) PFC James Gannone, PFC John Clements (wounded three times), and PFC Timothy Gahan.

Tim had learned to cut hair during his summers as a counselor at Camp Fatima. He brought a pair of barber clippers with him and gave haircuts to his brother Marines. He was the only one on the ship to have them. When word got out that he had clippers, he was called to the upper deck where NCOs (noncommissioned officers) and the few officers on the ship were billeted. "Do you have clippers and do you know how to cut hair?" Tim was asked. "Yes, sir!" So that is how he got the job to go to the upper deck and cut hair. Sometimes at the end of the day, he would get some fruit or other edible consideration for his services. He would gather up the fruit, take it below, and pass it out to his friends. Tim recalls, "I was well off. Others had far less desirable details: swabbing decks, cleaning heads, and squaring away the berthing stations. I had the best job of all my friends."

There was a brief stop at White Beach, Okinawa, to refuel. The senior Marine on the ship was a captain, and he wanted to let the men off the ship since they had been at sea so long. It would be difficult to check men off and on the ship and still allow time for some liberty. Tim remembers vividly, "We were all called on deck. The captain said, 'This is how it is: we will only be here a few hours, but we are going to let you go ashore.'" Tim recalled, "Everyone realized the importance of getting back in time, and wouldn't let the captain down. If something went wrong, the captain would be held responsible. We scrambled off the ship in high spirits. There was a small club near the beach, and in the matter of minutes it was sold out of cold beer. We all chipped in for a case of warm beer and headed to the beach. We stripped down to our skivvies and went for a swim. It was absolutely wonderful to lie in the sun and then go for a swim. More importantly, we all made it back to the ship in time. Everybody came back."

When the ship made port in Da Nang, Marines gathered their gear and disembarked in a drizzling rain. Roll was called, and everyone received their initial assignment. Tim was assigned to the Marine Aircraft Group 16, located at Marble Mountain Air Facility just south of Da Nang, with Marine Medium Helicopter Squadron 265. The billeting at MMAF was known as Southeast Asia huts. They were built a couple of feet off the ground with either canvas or corrugated tin roofs meant to house about a dozen men. There was one large mess hall on the base. It was open almost continuously in support of around-the-clock flight and maintenance operations.

When finished eating, the men would bring their mess kits and dinnerware to the cleaning stations outside the mess hall. There they would first empty the mess kits in a slop bucket, then go to a line of large barrels filled with hot water for washing and rinsing.

The outhouses at MMAF could accommodate four men at a time, and featured fifty-five-gallon steel drums cut in half, placed under holes that had been cut out of sheets of plywood. Periodically a crew pulled out the half-drums, soaked the contents with kerosene, and set them alight. You can imagine the stench! When the call of nature did not necessitate using an outhouse, a large-diameter screen-covered pipe sunk deep in the ground and rising about two feet above the surface was used. Showers at Marble Mountain consisted of a long warehouse with a series of pipes with fittings overhead.

LCpl Gahan outside Marine Medium Helicopter Squadron 265 headquarters, Marble Mountain Air Facility during the fall of 1966 on a rare day when it was not raining.

Tim reported to HMM-265 at MMAF in late September 1966. He was assigned to the squadron S-1 Section, a small group that provided administrative support for the unit. As the most junior and most recently arrived Marine, his initial posting was as mail orderly. It was the rainy season and the roads had been turned into muddy tracks, making travel difficult, especially by foot. When motor transport was not available, he had to walk miles in ankle-deep mud, sometimes twice a day, in the seemingly never-ending rain to and from the MMAF mail distribution center. His poncho was not much use in keeping him dry, and his leather boots were always soaked. One day while Tim was sorting mud-splattered mail, a postal inspector made a surprise visit to the squadron. There was much about the mail operation that was less than ideal, but the inspector took into account the conditions (water coming through a seam in the canvas overhead, using an ammunition crate to secure undeliverable mail, walking on pallets to keep out of the mud, etc.) and was thankfully more helpful than harsh in his findings. Tim thought perhaps his sorry appearance and being new to his duties influenced the inspector's leniency.

The tent on the right is the one in which Private First Class Gahan was sorting the mail when the postal inspector made his unannounced visit in October 1966.

Like most Marines assigned to noncombat duties, my brother wanted to serve a more active role in the war. When two openings to helicopter gunnery school became available, my brother and another Marine from the unit, a Puerto Rican American tent-mate from New York City, volunteered for the training. It was a weeklong program conducted at Camp Hansen, Okinawa. The training was on the M-60 machine gun and the aerial gunnery from UH-34D helicopters. HMM-265, Tim's unit, was equipped with the .50 caliber M2 machine gun, and flew CH-46A helicopters; but no matter, the training was transportable or transferable. The course was conducted over the Christmas and New Year holiday, and the respite in Okinawa was most welcome!

On return to the squadron, one of the two was to begin flying straight away and the other to replace him a month later, in February. The Marine from New York City began first. Only a short time later, the helicopter on which Tim's friend was the gunner was shot down while attempting to extract a reconnaissance team. The crew and the recon Marines were surrounded and spent the night fighting off the enemy until they could be rescued the following day. Tim remembered, "Late on the day they got out, I stopped by our hooch and was surprised to see my friend there alone sitting on the end of his bunk. He had been lightly wounded in the knee. I don't recall exactly what he said about the experience. He didn't say much, but his expression told me 'this machine gunner deal is for real.' I remember he was given the rest of the day off and went back to flying the next day."

Tim began flying missions as a helicopter machine gunner in February 1967. His tasks were to clean and service the two .50 caliber M2 machine guns on the aircraft; clean the barrier filters on the engine intakes; assist in refueling and loading; and do whatever the crew chief directed. When flying, he was to watch from his position on the port (left) side for anything unusual. He rotated from one aircraft to another, depending on the flight schedule. The missions included troop lifts, resupply, reconnaissance team insertions and extractions, and medical evacuations (medevacs). Most flights began at MMAF and returned there by the end of the day, but sometimes the crew would RON (remain overnight) elsewhere. Tim soon saw most all of I Corps, the northern region of the Republic of Vietnam.

On occasion he was assigned to a Sparrowhawk or Bald Eagle crew, who stood ready to launch with little notice. Later in the month he was assigned to the crew of EP 161 and was RON at Phu Bai, Khe Sanh, and Dong Ha for a time. While at Dong Ha on February 28, the pilot, Captain Lear, told his group, "Buckle up, this could get exciting."

Due to extremely hazardous conditions, Lear could have declined the mission. When asked later at the reunion, Captain Lear said that there was never any question—those Marines were in real trouble. Marines take care of Marines. Approaching the landing zone, Tim recalled, "They opened up on us from a number of positions all at the same time." The water and ammunition were dumped under heavy fire, and the helicopter lifted off and moved out of direct fire as quickly as possible. In any case, considerable damage was sustained by the aircraft. They limped home and arrived leaking hydraulic fluid. Tim was instructed to stay with the damaged helicopter until a maintenance contact team from the squadron could be sent to assess the damage to the aircraft. A few days later, the team arrived and determined the helicopter could not be repaired on site. A heavy lift helicopter, a "flying crane," was used to transport the heavily damaged helicopter to MMAF.

Years later, investigation showed that LCpl Jose Holguin from El Paso was killed in action at that location that night. In March a year earlier, Lance Corporal Gahan, who recently joined the Marines, left his hometown, El Paso, Texas. Tim was on the same flight and was in the same boot camp platoon as Holguin. As "homeboys," they naturally became friends. One time Tim was trying to encourage Jose to navigate a physically challenging station on an obstacle course. Tim was cheering him on in Spanish. The drill instructor put a quick stop to that, even though he was trying to be helpful to his friend. On another occasion, Jose and Tim were walking back to their hut from the "head." They were laughing and bumping into each other; you know, horseplay. The drill instructors were not amused, and both Tim and Jose were given extra PT for their roughhousing.

I remember my parents going to Jose Holguin's funeral in March 1967. It really struck close to home. What I could not know was the connection my family and the Holguin family would later have. In May 2019, my son Ted was in El Paso, Texas. While there he visited my parents' grave at the Fort Bliss National Cemetery and Jose Holguin's grave as well. We wanted to connect with Jose's family and let them know that his service to our country had not been forgotten. Ted not only placed flowers on his grave, but also placed a small piece of paper with his contact phone number and folded it up and taped it to the tombstone. Military cemeteries are well known for being neat and tidy, so we never thought anyone would see the flowers, much less find the small, folded note. Well, to our surprise, someone did find the note. It was Jose's brother, Abelardo, who was visiting the cemetery over that Memorial Day weekend. He first saw the flowers and called his sister Martha to ask if she had put them there. Then he noticed the small note. He immediately called my son, and was overwhelmed with making the connection.

Holguin's sister, Martha described how the family learned their brother was killed in action. A Marine Corps car drove up the driveway of the Holguin family home with Marine representatives and the family parish priest, Fr. Martinez. Jose's mother, Maria Holguin, was concerned and wanted to know what happened to her *hijo*. Upon hearing the news of his death, Mrs. Holguin began to sob. She had a heart condition, and her family brought her to the emergency room at the nearby hospital. Her daughter, Martha, said that her mother never got over the death of her firstborn son. Martha said, "We are a patriotic family. I can't believe that we made this connection to my brother on Memorial Day weekend. I have a flag flying at my home today." Martha sent a text attachment of a small poster that I will never forget. The poster read: "I was prepared to serve, I was prepared to be wounded, I was prepared to die. However, when I came home, I was not prepared to be forgotten!" LCpl Jose Holguin Jr. has not been forgotten.

Following the emergency resupply mission, Tim made his way back to his unit, and was then assigned to mess duty. He, another Marine, and a crew of about six Vietnamese were tasked with operating the mess kit cleaning stations outside the mess hall. The work was dirty and difficult, and the hours were long. It involved emptying slop buckets, scrubbing out and refilling washing barrels, and maintaining immersion burners to heat the water in the barrels. One day a bunker rat bit the other Marine, which excused him from mess duty because of an open wound in the hand. He was not replaced, making the work more arduous for my brother.

Tim established good relations with the Vietnamese and conversed with them in French. Most of them had fought with the French against the Communist Viet Minh in the early 1950s. They were curious about American life and would ask questions about living in the United States. Tim would occasionally give them packs of cigarettes and other small items, and allow them to take home whatever leftover food they liked. One of them invited him to his house for dinner. Tim thought it would be interesting but declined the offer, because being alone off the base at night was "unadvisable."

For a historical perspective, Vietnam had been a French colony from 1887 to 1954 except from 1941 to 1945, when the Japanese took over during World War II. The French influence was still present when Tim was in Vietnam, especially in language. In fact, the current Vietnamese script was developed by a French Jesuit missionary in the seventeenth century prior to the French colonial period. Tim's high school French classes and his time at Camp Fatima with French Canadians came in handy!

Tim recalled a night shortly after the squadron displaced from MMAF to Phu Bai, Tha Thien Province, in the spring of 1967. "We were far more concerned with unloading, unpacking and setting things up to support flight operations in our new location than working on ground defense. Sure enough, we came under mortar fire a night or two after our arrival and had no bunkers or trenches in which to take cover. I ran out of our tent and flattened myself along a nearby dirt track. During a short lull in the firing, I ran back to the tent, retrieved my rifle and a couple of loaded magazines, and went back to the slight depression I had just occupied. I remember being prone and making myself as small as possible with dirt and rock raining on me, praying the mortar fire would not be followed up by a ground attack. The next day, all hands who could be spared, myself included, were engaged in filling sandbags and constructing bunkers. We did so quickly and happily."

In his book *Bonnie-Sue, A Marine Corps Helicopter Squadron in Vietnam,* Marion Sturkey writes of that Phu Bai mortar attack. Two pilots were in their tents when blasts were heard. Tracers arced through the night. One of the pilots left the tent, tried to dig a hole with his hands so he could crawl into it. He finally abandoned his digging, leaped to his feet, and began running. He knew he had to get away. He found a gas tank that he crawled to, and hunkered down under it. Finally, the incoming mortars rounds stopped, and he made his way back to the tent. In the morning, the other pilot looked spiffy and totally refreshed. When questioned about the "rough night," they realized that the dapper pilot had peacefully slept through the entire mortar attack!

My brother remembered another incident that took place not long thereafter. "May Day, May 1, is the most important day on the international Communist calendar. On that day in 1967, a few Viet Cong guerrillas infiltrated an area between our flight line and the ARVN (Army of the Republic of Vietnam) camp to the north, and fired in both directions. A few of our troops ran to the armory for M-60 machine guns and ammunition and then set up positions along a berm facing the ARVN camp. After the Marines fired a few short bursts and some fire was received from the ARVN camp, a 'cease fire' order was received. Soon the word was passed, the VC (Viet Cong) wanted to initiate an 'intramural firefight' between our squadron and the ARVN camp, and the small enemy force withdrew after firing on both locations. Fortunately, no one was injured, but the incident made us more aware of potential dangers. Such was daily life."

On the left, Lance Corporal Gahan trying to look like a real Marine. Bunker in background was next to his tent. Phu Bai, May 1967. On the right, outside his tent packing up to leave Phu Bai to embark aboard the USS *Tripoli* (LPH 10). Tim ran from the tent during a mortar attack and landed in the slight depression along the edge of the track to his left.

In June, the squadron departed Phu Bai and became the air combat element of a Special Landing Force (SLF) operating from the USS *Tripoli* (LPH 10). The infantry component of the SLF was 2nd Battalion, 3rd Marines (BLT [Battalion Landing Team] 2/3). Life at sea was good. The berthing spaces were air conditioned, the men slept on clean sheets, and ice cream was available on the mess deck after hours. Tim, recently promoted to corporal, was the squadron clerk. The SLF operated along the coast of I Corps until late summer when BLT 2/3 offloaded. HMM-265 remained aboard the USS *Tripoli* when she sailed to Subic Bay, Philippines. After about a week in Philippines, the USS *Tripoli*, with the squadron aboard, returned to waters off Vietnam. Tim's unit offloaded in August at MMAF, the base it left some months before. Tim then became the courier between his unit and the squadron higher headquarters (Marine Aircraft Group 36) at Ky Ha, on the coast north of Chu Lai. He traveled with a satchel and pistol, and said he felt a bit like James Bond 007.

Aboard the USS *Tripoli* (LPH 10) in the summer of 1967 off the coast of
I Corps, Vietnam. Corporal Gahan is in the fourth row, sixth from the
right, bending forward. The Marine to his right is wearing sunglasses.
"Life was good on that ship."

My younger sister Madonna remembered, "During the nightly
news on TV I would listen and watch the action, and became
increasingly scared for Timmy. I remember one night awakening
from a nightmare about Timmy and the tragic events in the dream.
I went to mom and daddy's bedroom crying and woke them up,
telling them of the dream. I slept the rest of the night between mom
and daddy (in only a full-size bed, mind you), feeling secure and
saying the rosary."

I was a high school sophomore in 1967. My parents and six
brothers and sisters prayed constantly for Tim's safety. I was
attending Loretto Academy in El Paso, Texas. The Sisters of Loretto
and students regularly prayed for all our troops overseas. One of my
friends, Monica, had a special devotion to St. Joseph. Her aunt had
given a statue of St. Joseph to her years earlier, and Monica regularly

recited an ancient prayer to St. Joseph. When Monica heard my brother was serving in Vietnam, she handwrote the Prayer to St. Joseph, and I mailed it to him. Imagine my surprise when, a half century later, my brother, now Fr. Timothy Gahan, returned the prayer to me. He had kept it in a zipped plastic tobacco pouch along with his ID card, some MPC (military payment currency), dong (Vietnamese money), and a Geneva Convention card. That pouch protected the fragile paper from sweat, dirt, and rain. He carried it with him throughout his tour in Vietnam and prayed it regularly. The tattered paper with the barely legible handwritten prayer is now old, creased, and falling apart from continuous folding and unfolding. I reached out to my friend on her birthday in 2018 via social media. She was overwhelmed to know that the prayer she shared as a high school student was kept and meant so much to a Marine over half a century ago—a Marine who was later ordained to the priesthood.

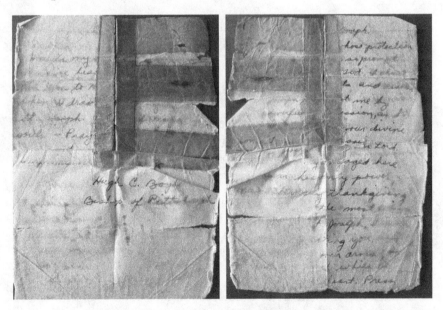

Handwritten Prayer to St. Joseph that was kept in a plastic tobacco pouch throughout my brother's tour in Vietnam. The barely legible, tattered paper is old, creased, and falling apart from continuous folding and unfolding for prayer.

Ancient Prayer to St. Joseph

> *Oh, St. Joseph, whose protection is so great, so strong, so prompt before the throne of God, I place in you all my interest and desires. Oh, St. Joseph, do assist me by your powerful intercession, and obtain for me from your divine Son all spiritual blessings, through Jesus Christ, our Lord. So that, having engaged here below your heavenly power, I may offer my thanksgiving and homage to the most loving of Fathers. Oh, St. Joseph, I never weary contemplating you, and Jesus asleep in your arms; I dare not approach while He reposes near your heart. Press Him close in my name and kiss His fine head for me and ask Him to return the kiss when I draw my dying breath. St. Joseph, patron of departing souls, pray for me. Amen.*

The old postscript to the St. Joseph prayer reads: "This prayer was found in the 50th year of our Lord and Savior Jesus Christ. In 1505, it was sent from the Pope to Emperor Charles when he was going into battle. Whoever shall read this prayer or hear it or keep it about themselves, shall never die a sudden death or be drowned, nor shall poison take effect on them, neither shall they fall into the hands of the enemy or be burned in any fire or be overpowered in battle. Say for nine mornings for anything you desire. It has never been known to fail." The prayer received an imprimatur in 1950 from the Bishop of Pittsburgh, Hugh Boyle.

This prayer was also prayed by many men in many wars across the centuries. Another Marine serving in Vietnam in 1971 remembers an army chaplain who was a Jewish rabbi, distributing the prayer on a card. He carried it with him for eighteen months. A craftsman was asked to frame a customer's French grandfather's pocket St. Joseph prayer card that the grandfather carried during World War II. The prayer was written in French.

In October 1967, Tim came home from Vietnam. True to his personality of being "Mr. Mischief," he surprised us all. My sister Madonna remembered, "The day he came back from Vietnam was certainly a celebratory occasion. It was a Sunday morning and we had just driven home from Mass. Before daddy could unlock the front door, Timmy opened it. I thought mom and daddy were going to have heart attacks. You see, Timmy wanted his homecoming to be a surprise, so he didn't tell anyone the details of his arrival. He apparently jimmied open a back window, crawled in the house, and waited for our return. After the hoopla died down, Timmy went to his bed and I believe he slept for three days straight! I know mom said we needed to keep quiet to let him sleep as long as he could."

Madonna also remembered: "One day, daddy and Timmy were sitting on the back patio. This was a few years after his return. They were talking in serious, hushed tones. As I stepped onto the patio, they both turned to look at me. I knew from their glances that I had walked into a deep discussion and should not intrude. I found out later they were talking with each other about war as only those that have participated can. What a special bond they had."

My sister Sheila remembered, "When Timmy visited us in Virginia only a week or so after his return, my husband Joe took him to see Colonial Williamsburg. He enjoyed it very much, but all of a sudden he heard rifle fire and dove for the ground—a natural instinct since he recently returned from Vietnam. The rifle fire came from the muskets fired by the 'colonial soldiers' during a reenactment. It was a reminder to all of us that Vietnam left an impact on all who served."

Tim's thoughts on Vietnam: "I was always proud of my service there, such as it was, and most especially of being a Marine . . . there's just something about the corps. I'm grateful for the experience. The men I was privileged to serve with in Vietnam were truly remarkable, and I was honored to be in their company. May God bless them all and the souls of our fallen comrades *requiescant in pace*."

Prayer to Saint Joseph

Oh, Saint Joseph, whose protection is so great, so strong, so prompt before the throne of God, I place in you all my interests and desires.

Oh, Saint Joseph, do assist me by your powerful intercession and obtain for me from your divine Son all spiritual blessings, through Jesus Christ, our Lord; so that having engaged here below your heavenly power, I may offer my thanksgiving and homage to the most loving of Fathers.

Oh, Saint Joseph, I never weary contemplating you, and Jesus asleep in your arms. I dare not approach while He reposes near your heart. Press Him in my name and kiss His fine head for me, and ask Him to return the kiss when I draw my dying breath. St. Joseph, patron of departing souls, pray for me. Amen.

Chapter Six

Back on Campus—Life is Good

Following a short leave after returning from overseas, Tim reported to the 5th Marine Division at Camp Pendleton, California, in November 1967. He was discharged in January 1968, and in a few days was back on a college campus. Only one week later the Tet Offensive, the largest campaign of the Vietnam War, began. The scale and extent of the fighting shocked the nation. Soon Tim learned that many Marines from his unit at Camp Pendleton suddenly found themselves en route to Vietnam, even those who, like himself, had only recently returned from there.

My brother planned on returning to college after being discharged from the Marines, and decided to attend North Texas State University (now the University of North Texas) in Denton, Texas. Why North Texas State? When Tim attended Cisco Junior College a few years earlier, he ran in track meets all over the state. He remembered when the track team went to North Texas State in Denton, there were girls who would come and watch them run. Most places did not draw many spectators, so Tim remembered these groups of "lovely ladies" and nearby Texas Woman's

University. North Texas State was a public school and relatively inexpensive.

My brother went to school on the GI Bill, which during this time was not as generous as it had been following World War II. He was paid $130 a month if he enrolled for fifteen semester hours or more of classes. During World War II, schools were tuition free up to $500, and veterans also received a cost-of-living stipend. My brother learned to live frugally and was able to graduate with no debt by working part-time periodically. In the spring of 1968, he lived in a dormitory, competed in intramural track, joined Phi Kappa Theta fraternity, and was president of his pledge class. Because of his background and that he was a year or two older than most of the fraternity brothers, he was never subjected to any fraternity pledge foolishness.

During the late sixties, NTSU was known as a big Texas party school, with "hippies," dope, and Vietnam War protests. However, there was also an active ex-Marine association, with veterans returning to school after serving their country. Events in the world included the siege of Khe Sanh and a man landing on the moon. The 1968 siege of Khe Sanh was the longest, deadliest, and most controversial battle of the Vietnam War, pitting the US Marines and their allies against the North Vietnamese Army. Lance Corporal Gahan had been there not long before the beginning of the siege.

During the summer of 1968, he lived in the Phi Kappa Theta fraternity house. In addition to his summer classes, he worked on the freight docks at Curtis Mathes TV in Dallas. In the fall, he played on the fraternity intramural football team as a lineman. In the spring of 1969, he moved to an off-campus apartment with a friend. The rent was $75 a month, which included utilities. It was an old house that had been divided up into five apartments.

Mary Patricia Hogan was a freshman at North Texas State in the fall of 1968. She had just graduated from Bishop Dunne High School in Dallas. That fall, a friend of Tim's whom Trisha went to high school with hosted a "welcome back to school" get-together. The girls who recently graduated from Bishop Dunne High School were invited. Mary Patricia, "Trisha" or "Trish," as she was known, attended. Tim had prior plans, but stopped briefly at the gathering to say hello, where he met Trisha. He was twenty-three and she was eighteen.

As Tim remembers, "She was quite good-looking, and there was something very attractive about her. She seemed to have it together. She was so nice. She never had an unkind word to say about anyone, and was always helping people. She was very smart and conscientious, very classy and well mannered. Not surprisingly, she was selected by the fraternity brothers as the Phi Kappa Theta Sweetheart in 1969."

The homecoming football game was approaching and Tim didn't have a date. He called Trisha. She declined, saying that she was going home that weekend. After they talked for a while, she admitted that other boys, including fraternity brothers, had also asked her to the homecoming game and dance and it would be awkward to go with him. So Tim said, "Tell your folks that it is homecoming, that you would like to stay, and I will take care of it on this end with the fraternity brothers." So she said yes. Little did she know that "yes" would change her life.

The summer of 1969 was a busy time, as he was attending summer school and had a job on the freight docks at Whitson Foods, and later was an orderly at Texas Woman's University, both in Denton. The TWU Research Institute conducted a study to determine the physiologic effect of long-term immobility. Pauline Beery Mack, PhD, director of TWU's Research Institute, served as a NASA investigator, specializing in bone density research. NASA selected Dr. Mack to conduct bed-rest studies on healthy men to evaluate the effects of inactivity on bone mass. There were a dozen men put to bed for ten weeks, and placed on a diet of food that astronauts would consume. Tim's duties were to empty bedpans and bag and tag the contents, serve food, make sure the heart monitors were functioning properly, supervise prescribed exercises in the bed, respond to participant requests, and keep the place clean and tidy.

The program participants were diverse in age and race. Tim remembers the men signed a contract before they entered the study; they were given about $1,000 at the start and another $1,000 at its completion. One man didn't show up on the first day of the study after receiving the initial $1,000! He was tracked down at the bus station and agreed to go back and fulfill his contract obligation.

In 1970, NASA's astronaut corps presented Dr. Mack with a Silver Snoopy, a distinguished honor given to NASA employees and contractors for excellence in support of the space missions and achievements related to improving space flight safety. Dr. Mack continued her bone density studies until her death in 1974. The bone density research performed remains relevant today as NASA continues to study the impact of long-term space travel.

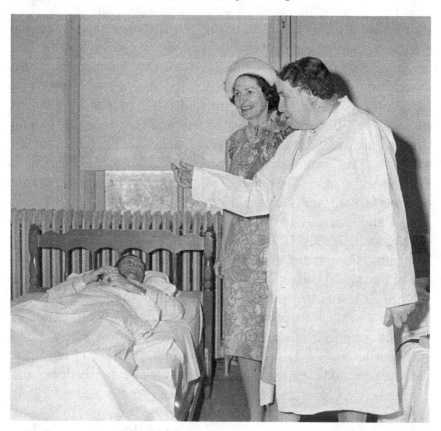

Dr. Pauline Beery Mack of Texas Women's University, Bone Density Study. Dr. Mack headed the NASA bed-rest experiment to determine the effects of prolonged immobilization. She is pictured with Lady Bird Johnson, the First Lady, visiting one of the men in the study in which Tim worked as an orderly during the summer of 1969. Photo courtesy of Getty Images/ Bettmann.

Who wants to be known as "the monkey guy"? The TWU Research Institute also had monkeys that were used periodically in space program research. At the end of the prolonged bed-rest study on men, Tim signed on to care for the monkeys on weekends during the fall. The pay was quite good, as was his pay for the bed-rest study, and helped a struggling veteran make ends meet while he shouldered a full academic load.

The monkeys were kept in cages in a small building on campus. Tim ensured they had food and water, cleaned the cages, and administered medications that were needed to study bone density. In order to get a monkey to digest the medicines, Tim needed to tranquilize him, pin the monkey against the cage door, pull his arms behind him, extract him from the cage, then force open and squirt the medication into his mouth with a syringe. The monkeys were remarkably intelligent, strong, and shifty. Sometimes they would only play at being sufficiently tranquilized and then rush the cage door when Tim opened it. Once one of the monkeys opened his own cage, something really quite impressive and totally unexpected. It required pushing aside a plate while pulling up a lever and lifting the locking bar all at the same time. When Tim opened the door to the building in which the cages were kept, the escaped monkey was above the doorway, ready to pounce. Tim had to call his fraternity brothers to help him get the monkey back into his cage. After that episode, my brother always made certain all monkeys were in their cages before opening the building door! At social gatherings that fall, Tim told many entertaining stories about his little mischievous friends, some of them were even true!

Imagine taking care of eight monkeys weighing about twenty to twenty-five pounds each dressed in little flight suits. Not long before Thanksgiving of 1969, about eight of the TWU Research Institute monkeys were used in another study. They were strapped into a frame in a slight reclining position so they could turn their heads to get a drink from a water bottle, and had forearms and lower legs free.

Tim took care of the monkeys on weekends and through the Thanksgiving and Christmas holidays. He would feed them food pellets with a pair of tongs after opening their mouths with a wooden dowel. Sometimes the monkeys would hide the pellets in their mouth and then spit the pellets out when Tim's back was turned. Tim became concerned the monkeys were not eating the food provided by the study, and when their health appeared to begin to fail, he fed them apple slices, which they found irresistible. That broke down their resistance to eating the pellets. Tim was alone with them from early morning until late at night. Often, he would read one of his college text books aloud, which seemed to interest them and had a calming effect on them. He spent Christmas Eve and all Christmas Day alone with the little fellows.

Tim has fond memories of North Texas State. He played intramural and Greek life sports, including football, basketball, swimming, and track and field. In the spring of 1968, he won the school intramural half-mile run. In the summer of the following year, when it was likely he would soon be going back into the Marines, he began to exercise in earnest. That fall he practiced with the NTSU cross-country team, and the coach arranged for him to have a locker, workout clothing, and participate in a few "at home" meets run on the NTSU golf course.

He drove a 1961 MGA convertible with all-leather interior. It was fun to drive but sometimes the passenger side door would latch and sometimes it wouldn't. Tim failed to mention this to my sister Sheila and her husband, Joe, when they visited him at North Texas State. Sheila remembered, "Tim was very proud of his little MGA sports car and wanted to take my husband Joe for a spin in it. Off they went, zooming around the corner, and the door flew open! Joe almost flew out of it!"

On the left, North Texas State, fall 1968. On the right, with his 1961 MGA 1600 Roadster, fall 1969. Note the USMC decal.

Tim graduated in January 1970 with a bachelor of science degree in physical education and minor in speech. Even before returning from overseas Tim had decided to return to college on expiration of his enlistment, and pursue a commission in the Marine Corps. The sense of doing something much larger than himself appealed to him. Tim recalls, "I really enjoyed the camaraderie, esprit de corps, and challenging yourself. The Marines are a unique organization. I wanted to have another go at it. Last time I served as an enlisted man. I thought it should help with leadership, having a couple of years' experience within the ranks. I wanted to go back to the brotherhood."

When my brother graduated from North Texas State University, there was a gap between graduation and starting the Marine Officer Candidate School (OCS) class. Tim had already sold his famous car, vacated his apartment, given away most of his clothes, and said his goodbyes. This delay gave him a month to go back to El Paso, where he coached track and field at Burges High School as a volunteer. He had graduated from Burges seven years earlier.

Tim flew out the first week of March 1970 to Quantico, Virginia, and graduated from OCS at the end of May. Mom and dad attended the commissioning, along with Trisha. Trisha's mother and father met my parents at the Dallas airport as they were en route to Quantico. Graduation was on a Friday, and my mom and Trisha pinned the second lieutenant bars on Tim's shoulders. Everyone got a chuckle when Trisha initially pinned the bars the wrong way. After the commissioning, on Saturday, they all traveled to Williamsburg to spend the weekend. Tim and Trisha were not engaged at the time, so it was a perfect opportunity for everyone to get to know one another.

On the left, at Marine Corps Base Quantico, May 1970. Our mother and Mary Patricia (Trisha) pinning on second lieutenant bars. On the right, 2ndLt Timothy M. Gahan at the Basic School, Camp Barrett, Marine Corps Base Quantico, summer 1970.

Madonna recalled, "I always remember Timmy having a girl by his side—quite the ladies' man he was. All the girls were beautiful as I recall, but the most beautiful was Mary Patricia Hogan (Trisha). I remember when mom and dad went for the Marine officer commissioning for Tim. When mom and dad came home, Mom kept going on and on about Trisha—'Beautiful girl! So sweet and kind.' What a blessing to our family!"

After commissioning, there were six more months of training at Quantico, Virginia, at the Marine Basic School. In November, after training, Tim traveled to Dallas, where he was assigned temporary duty. Newly commissioned officers could request duty at a recruiting office for up to thirty days. He talked to prospective candidates for OCS traveling to colleges within Texas and southern New Mexico.

Tim asked Trisha to marry him during the long Labor Day weekend in Dallas. He had a beautiful solitaire diamond engagement ring ready, and she said, "Yes!" Years later, when Tim was ordained to the priesthood, he had that solitaire diamond embedded in his chalice. The chalice features a Celtic design cross, which was created by cutting Tim's wedding ring into two pieces and flattening them to form the cross, and Trisha's wedding ring was set as the circular element of the cross. The diamond from her engagement ring was mounted in the center of the cross.

Fr. Gahan's chalice with Celtic cross created with Tim's and Trisha's wedding rings. The diamond from Trisha's engagement ring is mounted in the center of the cross.

Chapter Seven

Semper Fi, Part II

On a mild evening a week before Christmas 1970, Mary Patricia Hogan and 2ndLt Timothy Mannix Gahan were married at a nuptial Mass at St. Cecilia Roman Catholic Church in Dallas, Texas. It was a beautiful event complete with a traditional Marine sword arch. Trisha's two sisters were among the bridesmaids, and Tim's two brothers were best man and a groomsman.

2ndLt Timothy Mannix Gahan and Mary Patricia (Hogan) Gahan at wedding reception, December 1970.

Tim and Trisha enjoyed a Christmas honeymoon in the scenic mountains of Cloudcroft, New Mexico, where they stayed in a small mountain cabin. The cabin was so rustic that when Tim tried to light the gas stove, it blew up, sending him flying across the room. There was no major damage, but his eyebrows were singed off. A few days later, they visited Tim's parents in nearby El Paso. Then on to Tim's first duty station at Camp Pendleton, California.

Tim's first assignment was platoon commander, Weapons Platoon, Company M, 3rd Battalion, 3rd Marines, 5th Marine Amphibious Brigade. The battalion was located at Camp San Mateo at the northern end of Camp Pendleton, by chance the same camp at which Tim underwent infantry training in the summer of 1966. By further coincidence, his platoon was billeted in the same barracks and in the very squad bay in which he had been assigned four and a half years earlier. Even more remarkable was that his small makeshift platoon office was on the very spot where his rack had been located! Three months later, his unit was redesignated Weapons Platoon, Company M, 3rd Battalion, 7th Marines, 1st Marine Division. The redesignation was prompted by the return of 1st Marine Division to Camp Pendleton, California, from Vietnam as part of the American draw down from Vietnam.

While stationed at Camp Pendleton, Trisha was a volunteer for the Navy Relief Society and at the Oceanside Library. In November, Tim received orders for Okinawa, Japan. As an unaccompanied tour he had to leave his new wife, now expecting their first child, stateside.

Trisha returned to North Texas State University in Denton, Texas, to continue studies, and in the summer of 1972, moved home to Dallas, living in the guest cottage. In the meantime, Tim was assigned as training officer for Supply Battalion, 3rd Force Service Regiment at Camp Foster, Okinawa.

In May 1972, he shipped out to Nam Phong, Khon Kaen Province, Thailand. He was part of Logistical Support Group Delta, providing support to the squadrons operating out of the newly established expeditionary airfield. Since conditions were primitive, the base soon earned the nickname the "Rose Garden" after the then popular song by Lynn Anderson. The Marines capitalized on it and developed a recruiting campaign with the slogan: "We don't promise you a rose garden," with a poster depicting a stern-looking Marine drill instructor addressing a terrified recruit nose to nose.

Marine recruiting campaign slogan, May 1972. The base at Nam Phong, Khon Kaen Province, Thailand earned the nickname the "Rose Garden" after the popular song and slogan.

LSG Delta provided airfield support during Operation Linebacker 72, the codename of a United States aerial bombing campaign conducted against targets of the Democratic Republic of Vietnam (North Vietnam). The operation resulted in restarting peace talks and halting the Easter Offensive, which was a military campaign conducted by the People's Army of Vietnam (PAVN) against the Republic of Vietnam (ARVN, the regular army of South Vietnam).

Terence Hogan Gahan was born in August of 1972 in Dallas, while Tim was deep in the jungles of northeast Thailand. He didn't know for some days about Terence's birth, as communication was very primitive. The Red Cross first sent the message to Tim's parent organization in Okinawa, who in turn notified him in Thailand.

Being a half a world apart, with limited communication, how do parents decide on a name? Trisha and Tim wrote to each other with lists of potential names, leaving a comment section where each could write in their thoughts. Terence's middle name was decided on first. Of the nine children in our Gahan family, only one had a family name as a middle name. Tim's middle name *Mannix* is our grandmother Gahan's family name. So they decided on Hogan, Trisha's family name, as the middle name for their firstborn. Terence was a name that kept appearing on the favorite list, so it was selected. After birth, when the nurse was confirming the newborn's name with Trisha, who recently delivered Terence, the nurse stated "Clarence." That certainly alerted Trisha, who quickly corrected the name!

In October 1972, Tim took a short leave to meet his newborn son in Dallas. At the end of his leave, he returned to Thailand. In early January 1973, Tim returned to Dallas, having completed his yearlong deployment. He had orders to return to Camp Pendleton; however, while on leave in Dallas, he received a phone call from the personnel assignment officer offering a slot in Hawaii. Tim said, "Let me discuss this with my wife." The scheduler stated he really needed an answer straightaway. Tim held his hand over the phone receiver and asked Trisha, "So, you want to go to Hawaii? They need an answer now." Trisha said, "Yes! That would be wonderful!" So off they went, leaving heavy coats, fur caps, wool scarves, and gloves in storage.

My brother was assigned to the Marine Barracks, Naval Ammunition Depot, Oahu. The Marine Barracks consisted of three detachments. The initial posting for Tim was as guard officer at Waikele. Six months later he was transferred to West Loch on Pearl Harbor, where he was the officer in charge of the security detachment. Tim remembers, "We had really nice quarters on Pearl Harbor. It came with a private fishpond, a crab pond, and a small boat. The quarters at West Loch were built with poured concrete walls because we were in the 'blast zone.' Ammunition was stored in igloos in the vicinity of the home, so all buildings required construction to withstand a potential blast. The backyard had plumeria, mango, and papaya trees." Many mornings they would walk through their yard, pick ripe sweet papaya, cut it in half, and scoop out the seeds. One half was used as a bowl for their breakfast cereal, and the other half used as an ice cream bowl for dessert that evening. Trash cans in Hawaii with swinging lids had the word "Mahalo" on them. Trisha thought "mahalo" was the word for trash. After living there six months, she finally realized the word is Hawaiian for "thank you!"

While in Hawaii, Tim took up distance running in events sponsored by the local Road Runners Club. He ran the Honolulu Marathon in 1973. The following year, the Security Team from West Loch participated a 140-mile relay race around Oahu. It took a lot of planning, with runners dropping off every mile or two. They also participated in the Kolekole Pass relay race. That relay was fifty-three miles starting at the ammunition depot, then up into the mountains, and finishing at Schofield Barracks. The views along the route were magnificent.

During their three years in Hawaii, the Gahan family took advantage of going to the beach often. Ewa Beach was the closest and one of their favorites. If they ever asked, "What are we doing this weekend?" They could always answer, "Let's go to the beach." The weather was beautiful, and they loved relaxing, lying in the sun. Another favorite pastime was visiting the Honolulu Zoo, which included seeing the starving-artist artwork displayed on the zoo fence. Some of these oil paintings were really excellent and inexpensive, so they picked up a few.

While in Hawaii, Trisha and Tim enjoyed entertaining guests at Fort De Russy Officer Mess, the Cannon Club, Honolulu. The club was built overlooking Honolulu and Waikiki Beach in 1945, and club membership was reserved for military officers. Unfortunately, it closed in 1997. A fire destroyed it under suspicious circumstances in 2003. They also hosted visitors at nearby Hickam Air Force Base Officers Club, which had a first-rate Mongolian barbecue buffet, and some nights featured fresh king crab legs. It overlooked Pearl Harbor, and being an Air Force Base, was also not open to the public.

The Waipio Peninsula separated West Loch from the western part of Pearl Harbor. In World War II it was used mostly to berth ammunition ships. To facilitate loading and unloading, piers were constructed along the peninsula. In May 1944, an explosion rocked West Loch when six LSTs (landing ship tanks) and three smaller landing crafts were destroyed. While stationed at West Loch, Tim's family would take their little boat and explore the rusted shipwrecks.

Tim remembers, "We had about seventy troops on 1,600 acres right on Pearl Harbor. It was a great assignment. In our first eighteen months, we had twenty-two houseguests, mostly family. Trisha made little packets and had brochures ready for visitors, with planned itineraries depending on what folks wanted to do and see." When our sister Sheila and her husband Joe visited the Gahan family in Hawaii in 1973, there was a severe gas shortage on the island. Tim and Trisha insisted they borrow their car to go to the Polynesian Cultural Center and see other sights as well. This entailed them getting up in the wee hours of the morning and sitting in a long line at the gas station to get the rationed gas. Who else would bend over backward for guests like that? But Tim and Trish were like that; if they could help in any way, they would do so.

One day in the summer of 1975, Trisha was putting leis together with leaves from the plumeria tree in their yard. She would pass a needle with dental floss through the stems, which had a milky sap. The next morning, when she awoke with a blurry eye, she thought perhaps some of the sticky substance got in her eye when she brushed her hair back with her hand. When it did not clear up, she visited an ophthalmologist who referred her to a neurologist for a consultation. After examination and testing, the neurologist walked into the room where Trisha and Tim were waiting and sat down. He explained the testing and exams confirmed his fears: she had multiple sclerosis, a neurological disease that has no cure. Things went along with little effect for a while. But over time, more symptoms began manifesting themselves. Tricia was twenty-five years old and pregnant with their second child when she was diagnosed. Her health declined rapidly, and a few years later she was confined to a wheelchair.

Kathleen Rose was born in September 1975 at Tripler Army General Hospital. The hospital was known as the "Pink Lady." During World War II, when the hospital needed to be painted, only a limited amount of red and white paint was available. The paints were mixed, and voilà! A pink hospital. It has been painted pink ever since.

In preparation for the birth, Tim attended childbirth classes with Trisha. All was well that Thursday night as they retired for the evening, and the weekend was in sight. That was all about to change. Early Friday morning, September 26, just after midnight, Trisha woke Tim and told him the time had come and they needed to go to the hospital. When they arrived at the hospital, nurses put Tricia in a wheelchair and scurried her off to an OB room. Tim was right behind. Once in the OB room, Tim ripped his shirt off, put on his scrubs, and threw the shirt underneath the gurney. Shortly afterward, they rolled Trisha on the gurney into the delivery room. Katie was born in the early hours. Tim remembers the doctor announcing, "It's a girl!" and Trisha was so happy. After the delivery, they rolled Trisha on the gurney into the recovery room. It was then that Tim realized his shirt was still under the gurney. So early in the wee hours, he tracked down the recovery room. It was a big room with several women recovering from giving birth. Trisha was way in the back, up making the bed. Tim remembers, "I tiptoed across the room with no shirt on, when a lady woke up, then another woke up, and another, resulting in quite a commotion—there was a half-dressed man in the room! Trisha quickly grabbed my shirt and threw it at me! I was a sight, running out of the recovery room bare chested with a shirt in my hand. On my way home that morning, the sun was just beginning to come up over Pearl Harbor. A truly magnificent sight and a cherished reminder of the beautiful day my daughter was born."

Trisha's mother stayed the first few days, then the young family settled into a regular routine. With a three-year-old and a newborn, "regular routine" can only be defined as controlled chaos. One day Terence tiptoed into baby Katie's room, reached in the crib, and pulled Katie out. Holding her in his arms, he walked proudly into the living room. He was all smiles, very happy with himself, having taken his sister on a "field trip." Trisha thought, "I must stay calm so Terence doesn't drop her!" Thankfully, it all worked out.

In January 1976, the Gahan family said *aloha* to Hawaii and moved to Quantico, Virginia, where Tim was assigned as officer in charge of the Range Unit, Weapons Training Battalion. In August he was reassigned as a student at the Amphibious Warfare School. They lived on base, which was enjoyable as all Tim's classmates lived nearby and the young families had much in common. They have wonderful memories of that place and time.

When Trisha's aunt Laura found out that Tim was to be stationed in Virginia, she gave Trisha a box of memorabilia of Trisha's great-grandfather, Patrick Hogan from Virginia, who fought in the Civil War. Trisha researched her family's history in nearby Washington, DC, and discovered Patrick Hogan served as a Confederate officer in the famous Stonewall Brigade. He had seen action in many battles, was wounded three times, and captured at the Battle of the Bloody Angle at Spotsylvania Courthouse. He was one of the Immortal 600, a group of 600 Confederate officers held prisoner in 1864–1865. Patrick survived the ordeal, and following the war, moved to Texas.

Upon completion of the Amphibious Warfare School, Tim and family returned to Camp Pendleton, California, where he was assigned as the assistant operations and training officer of the 7th Marines. A year later he was reassigned as commanding officer of Company C, 1st Battalion, 7th Marines. This was the same company in which he served as a platoon leader years earlier. The company conducted amphibious training at Coronado, mountain warfare training near Bridgeport, amphibious assaults at the beaches of Camp Pendleton, and numerous live-fire exercises. The Gahan family lived on base, overlooking the beach just south of San Clemente.

Capt. Timothy M. Gahan, commanding officer, Company C, 1st Battalion, 7th Marines, Camp Pendleton, spring 1979.

Following selection to major, Tim transferred to the Marine Corps Logistics Base, Barstow, California. He was the manpower management officer for the 2,000 civilian employee workforce, and the following year was reassigned as commanding officer, Headquarters Battalion. At night he attended Chapman University graduate school and earned a master of science degree in education, curriculum and instruction.

Barstow, "crossroads to the west," is located in the high desert. Always the athlete, Tim participated in numerous mini triathlons, road races, and enjoyed playing racquetball. He became a member of the Knights of Columbus, a Catholic fraternal organization, just as our dad had been all his adult life. Trisha was an active room mother at the Mt. St. Joseph Catholic School, the school Katie and Terence attended.

Tim returned to Quantico, Virginia, as a student at the Command and Staff College from 1983 to 1984. Following graduation, he remained at Quantico and was posted to the Marine Corps Leadership Department, where he contributed to writing manuals and materials for leadership programs. One of the more interesting things in which he participated was the production of a film on combat leadership. He was the technical advisor to the movie *Combat Leadership: The Ultimate Challenge*.

The vital importance of leadership on the battlefield has been demonstrated over the years. There are leadership traits and skills that have withstood the test of time in combat. The movie premiered at the 1987 Marine Corps Leadership Conference at Quantico. A diverse group was recruited for the movie. Veterans of WWI, the Banana Wars, WWII, Korean War, Vietnam, and Grenada were included. Some had served in combat in different ground occupational specialties, and others in air combat. Some were junior enlisted men, some NCOs, and others junior and senior officers. Actor and USMC veteran Lee Marvin narrated the film. During World War II, he was wounded and spent a year in a hospital. Marvin was pleased to be working again with Marines. This was the last movie he made. He was professional and easy to work with even though experiencing physical challenges. The production crew would have everything ready to film and then call him on set. When he was on camera, he rose to the occasion and amazed all.

The film featured Joe Foss, two-time governor of South Dakota and WWII Medal of Honor recipient; and E. B. Sledge, author of the World War II memoir *With the Old Breed: At Peleliu and Okinawa*. The movie can still be viewed on YouTube: *Marine Corps Combat Leadership Skills*.

During his time at the Marine Corps Leadership Department, Gahan was technical advisor to the movie *Combat Leadership: The Ultimate Challenge* narrated by USMC WW II veteran Lee Marvin.

The Gahan family moved from Quantico base housing to a home in Fredericksburg, Virginia, in 1984. Trisha continued to fail physically and required assistance. This move provided housing for live-in help for her. Before moving in, several renovations were needed to make the home handicap accessible. My brother Ted, a skilled craftsman and experienced in renovations, drove to Virginia from Ohio to help out. Without prior notice, he arrived on Tim's doorstep. "Here I am. Let's go to work!" he announced. The trunk of his car was full of tools. He started knocking down walls to widen the bathroom entrance and then making an outdoor wheelchair ramp among other construction projects that the brothers did together to make the home suitable. It was a bonding moment for them; brotherly love in action.

Every few years our geographically scattered family gets together for boisterous family time. In the summer of 1985, the Gahan reunion took place at Fredericksburg, Virginia. All eight brothers and sisters and their families attended, as well as our mother. Our father, Col. Theodore P. Gahan (USA Ret), passed away in 1978. Trisha was discharged from Walter Reed Medical Center during the reunion. She was bedbound at this point, with leg contractures, difficulty seeing, and on a feeding tube for nutrition. When she arrived home in a makeshift ambulance in the back of the family SUV, she looked at me and said, "Oh, Colleen, I am so happy!" Her hospital bed at home was situated looking out large sliding glass doors to a big backyard with flowers and trees. My daughter Erin, who is Tim and Trisha's goddaughter, says, "I remember Aunt Trisha in her bed and we each went up to her and held her hand. I remember her lifting her head up to see us and her big smile."

The highlight of our reunion was the last night. We had a relaxed cookout at Tim's home, followed by Mass. Trisha's bed was in the middle of the room, with all of us around her. What blessings flowed that evening.

Chapter Eight

Trisha

How does a young wife and mother cope with a crippling and incurable progressive illness? Mary Patricia Hogan Gahan answered that question by keeping faith and trust in God, imploring the intercession of the Blessed Virgin Mary, and demonstrating more concern for others than herself.

Tim's favorite picture of Trisha

Mary Patricia Hogan was born in Dallas in 1950 to George H. and Helen L. (Dennehy) Hogan. "Trisha" attended grammar school at St. Cecilia Catholic School, followed by Bishop Dunne High School, a diocesan Catholic high school. Her younger sister Eileen remembers, "Sr. Benita Frances was the principal of St. Cecilia School. For some reason, we were all terrified of her. Trisha was the only one not scared of her. I think Trisha was one of Sister's favorites. Trisha was an excellent student, with proper manners, and a certain maturity that attracted others. I think that Trisha was born when she was forty because she was so mature for her age compared to everyone else."

Trisha was the eldest of the four Hogan children, followed by Kevin, Eileen, and Peggy. Eileen adored her and recalled, "She was my best friend in the whole world. We were really close. Whatever Trisha did, it was the coolest. I wanted to be like her when I grew up."

The three Hogan girls shared a large bedroom. Eileen and Trisha shared a double bed and younger sister Peggy had a twin bed. There was one closet shared by the three girls. Trisha and Eileen's big bed was old, with uncovered coil box springs. Sometimes if the girls were horsing around the bed would collapse on the floor. If the girls were joking and laughing, their dad would often remind them to hush. At night while lying in bed together, Eileen and Trisha would look out the window at the moon and try to make shapes where the old paint was on the window. The shadows could look like a man or giraffes. Always looking out for others, Trisha promoted and supported all the school activities, including novenas, Mass, and fundraising for charities.

Trisha's firm foundation in her faith would serve her well in coping with her multiple sclerosis. In 1983, while living in Barstow, California, as her health deteriorated, she was forced to use a wheelchair. Having a strong faith and devotion to the Blessed Mother, Tim and Trisha decided to make a pilgrimage to Lourdes, France; and Fatima, Portugal, both sites of Marian apparitions. Many miracles had been performed at both places, especially Lourdes. And with fervent prayer, maybe one would be granted for Tricia. Just maybe.

In the summer of 1983, while Terence and Katie were at summer camp, Tim and Trisha flew to Lisbon, Portugal. On arrival they rented a car and drove seventy miles north to Fatima. Along the way they saw thatched-roof roadside stands, many motorbikes, men in Scally caps, and donkey and ox carts on the two-lane road. Fatima became widely known in May 1917 when the Blessed Mother appeared to three shepherd children: Lucia dos Santos and her cousins Francisco and Jacinta Marto. The Miracle of the Sun is reported to have occurred there on October 13, 1917. Witnesses said they saw extraordinary solar activity: the sun, emitting radiant colors, appeared to "dance" or zigzag in the sky and careen toward the earth. Since then, thousands have made the pilgrimage to this holy site. Many physical cures attributed to the Pilgrim Statue of Our Lady of Fatima have been documented.

While at Fatima, they prayed at the Basilica of Our Lady of the Rosary, then Tim pushed Trisha in the wheelchair to the site of the apparition. At the entrance of the shrine, knee pads were available for pilgrims to walk on their knees in reverence while praying. Tim walked on his knees about forty yards at the site. He remembers, "I was praying that through Our Blessed Mother, under her title of Our Lady of Fatima, that Trisha and I would have a fruitful pilgrimage experience." That evening they went to bed listening to the chanting from the Fatima shrine.

Following the visit to Fatima, they left for Lourdes, France. Late on the first travel day they realized they would not be able to reach Salamanca, where they had hotel reservations. It was getting late when they saw a billboard advertising "Hotel Exe Alfonso VIII, Plasencia, Spain." It advertised "air-conditioning." The car had no air-conditioning and they were hot and tired, so the decision was made to stay at what turned out to be a wonderful hotel, oozing with old-world charm, in the heart of the town. Immediately after escorting them to their room, the hotel staff brought them a large silver tray on which were a full ice bucket, bottles of chilled mineral water, lovely stemware, and most welcome of all, a large pitcher of fresh sangria. Shortly thereafter they delivered a tray of delicious hors-d'oeuvres. Trisha and Tim got much needed rest that night.

The next morning, they continued their journey to Lourdes. After a long drive through the mountains of southern France, they arrived at Lourdes near midnight. As soon as they stopped at the hotel, Hotel Excelsior, the doorman immediately stepped out and said, "Mr. Gahan?" Tim replied, "Yes." The doorman said, "We have been expecting you, sir." Immediately, he assisted with the bags. Tim eased Trisha into the wheelchair, and to the room they went. The hotel was ideally located, with easy access to the Lourdes shrine and even had a small balcony on which one could enjoy morning coffee with a lovely view of the shrine.

The first day, Tim wheeled Trisha to the beautiful Marian shrine of Our Lady of Lourdes. The village of Lourdes is situated in the foothills of the Pyrenees Mountains. Bernadette Soubirous, a young peasant girl, reported Marian apparitions at Lourdes in 1858. Mary identified herself as "the Immaculate Conception" and gave a message for all: "Pray and do penance for the conversion of the world."

Since 1859, there have been seventy verified miracles or cures at Lourdes. As medical experts review the cases, they have to be absolutely certain there are no medical explanations for the cures. The most recent miracle was in 2008, when Sr. Bernadette Moriau of

France was cured of a neurological problem where she had difficulty walking, used medical aids, and was in constant pain. After visiting Lourdes, her cure was sudden, instantaneous, complete, and lasting.

Pools are filled with water from the spring flowing from the grotto at the site of the apparitions. Trisha would soon be immersed in one of those pools. The next morning, Tim pushed Trisha in her wheelchair to the Lourdes Grotto. As it came in sight, they saw two lines of scores of people. One line was for men, another for women. Rather than wait in a long line in the hot sun, they decided to visit other sites at the shine. They came upon a small office where officials investigate the miracles through the intersession of the Blessed Mother. Tim remembered, "We spoke with one of the doctors. He investigated reports of miraculous cures. He asked about Trisha's condition and if she had been to the grotto spring. We explained that we had just passed the spring, it had a long line, and we would not be able to physically wait long enough to bathe in it. He then said, 'Wait a moment,' excused himself, and came back with a small card, wrote something on it, then pinned it to Trisha's dress. 'Try this,' he said. Later we returned to the grotto. As we approached it, a group of young volunteers from Scotland wearing kilts walked quickly toward us. One of the volunteers read the card pinned to Tricia's dress. They immediately took Trisha straight to the front of the line. They told me where she would be when she finished taking the bath."

When Trisha came out, she told Tim the story of how she was put on a gurney with a sheet over her. Underneath the sheet, four or five women disrobed her, then rolled the gurney and immersed her in the waters of the spring. Trisha described, "When I came out of the water, I was completely dry!" She was redressed under the sheet, assisted back into her wheelchair, and rolled back to Tim, waiting nearby. Later that evening, they joined in the lighted candle procession singing Marian hymns. While there, they went to daily Mass and prayed numerous rosaries. They spent four glorious days there, and cherished every moment.

Years later, Fr. Gahan gave a homily about their trip to Lourdes, and how all prayers are heard.

Mark 5:21–43, "Do not be afraid; just have faith."

Our gospel reading this morning describes two miracles: the restoration of Jairus' daughter, and the cure of a woman afflicted with hemorrhages. Both are examples of faith in Christ's benevolence and omnipotence, for only a miracle could have returned them to good health. Just as both Jairus and the woman had complete faith that the Divine Physician could and would save the daughter and the woman who suffered greatly, we too should have faith that God will help us overcome the obstacles to salvation: Do not be afraid; just have faith.

Normally, God's help comes to us in an unspectacular way, but we should not doubt that if it is necessary for our salvation, God will work miracles for us, often in ways completely unexpected. The narrative reminded me of a young woman who had an incurable and often fatal neurological disease. She prayed fervently that she might be cured, or that at least she be spared of the worst effects of the disease until her ten-year-old son and seven-year-old daughter were young adults. The cause of the disorder was unknown and she underwent many different and sometimes arduous medical treatments to arrest the steady decline in her health. She received excellent care but the progression of the disease continued unabated. All the while she maintained a positive attitude and stormed the heavens with prayer. She had an especially strong devotion to Our Blessed Mother, the mediatrix of all graces, and implored her unfailing help. She and her husband knew that any improvement would require a miracle, so they went to Lourdes in southern France, site of many miraculous medical cures worked through the intercession of the Blessed Virgin. She bathed in the miraculous waters flowing from the spring located in the grotto there; prayed rosaries fervently;

attended holy Mass when her condition permitted; meditated at the imposing and inspiring basilica; went to confession; emptied herself to the Lord; and grew ever closer to the Mother of God during her stay at that holy place. She was in pain and tired easily, but never complained. She struggled physically, but her pretty face radiated peace and joy. It was as if she had a foretaste of heaven. The woman did not experience a physical miracle at Lourdes, but she did not seem disappointed. On the contrary, on the day of her departure her sweet face was glowing. There was silence in the car as she and her husband drove slowly away from a place she had grown to love and that she knew she would never again visit. After a time she asked her husband if he was disappointed, and he replied one could never be disappointed in Lourdes. He was startled when she told him a miracle had been performed . . . but not the one both had sought. The young mother explained the miracle was greater than restoration to good health as in the case of Jairus' daughter and the woman suffering from hemorrhages in our gospel reading. She told him she was most grateful for what she had experienced at the place and perfectly content. Her prayers had been answered but in a way she did not expect. She said she thought she had been given the grace and strength to accept God's will in her life unconditionally . . . and went on to say that while there, she found herself praying more and more in thanksgiving for the many blessings in her short life than for her cure. And asked that if a miracle were to take place that it be performed for another whose condition was more desperate than her own. She was happy.

I tell you this story to illustrate that all prayer, even prayer for miracles, is heard, but often answered in ways we do not expect. Many times, the reply exceeds what we requested, although sometimes it's quite difficult to understand how. The Gospel of St. Luke records Our Savior saying, "And I tell you, ask and you will receive; seek and you will find; knock and the door will be opened to you. For everyone who asks, receives; and the one who seeks, finds; and to the one who knocks, the door will be opened. What father among you would hand his son a snake when he asks for a fish? Or hand him a scorpion when he asks for an egg? If you then, who are wicked, know how to give good gifts to your children, how much more will the Father in heaven give the Holy Spirit to those who ask him?"

After returning home the young woman continued to fail but the joy of Lourdes, the resignation to accept and do God's will, the tender love of the Blessed Mother, and her great faith remained strong . . . indeed, it grew stronger still. The young, much loved wife and mother died two years later.

When Tim and Trisha planned their Marian pilgrimage, they shared the news with Trisha's parents. When Trisha was in high school, the Hogan family hosted a scientist from Poland, Kazik Przewlocki. He lived in the Hogan's guesthouse behind their home. He was from Krakow, Poland, an engineer, and part of a scientific exchange program. Years later, in correspondence with him, Mrs. Hogan mentioned that Tim and Trisha were going to Lourdes and Fatima. Dr. Przewlocki personally knew Pope John Paul II, and suggested the couple meet His Holiness if they came to Rome following their pilgrimage to Fatima and Lourdes. Dr. Przewlocki and his wife had dinner with the pope during the pope's second visit to Poland in the spring of 1983. There he mentioned Trisha to the Holy Father, and arrangements were made for an audience with him.

After the Fatima and Lourdes visits, they departed for Rome. Along the way, they stayed in Nice on the Riviera. When they arrived in the Eternal City, they phoned the monsignor who was their contact for the papal audience. It was July and the pope was at his summer residence, Castel Gandolfo, outside Rome. During this time, he only came to the Vatican on Wednesdays for audiences. The monsignor instructed Tim to go to one of the Vatican gates and clear a couple of Swiss Guard stations. Tim went as directed and found himself looking at a Swiss Guard seated at a desk on an elevated platform, with a stack of envelopes in front of him. The guard looked through the stack at least twice, searching for the Gahan name, and could not find it. Then he noticed two envelopes on the side of his desk, and there found the Gahan invitation to meet His Holiness, Pope John Paul II. The Swiss Guard stood, walked around the desk, and personally gave the invitations to Tim. The invitation was *Primera Fila*, meaning "first row," to have a personal encounter with the successor to St. Peter.

Upon arrival at the Vatican the next day, they received a brief orientation on security and proper protocol, such as staying seated and not attempting to make any sudden motions. There had been an attempt on the life of the pope just two years earlier, so security was especially important. Finally, the moment came when Pope John Paul II was standing before them. The gentleman on Trisha's right spoke German, so when the pope came to Trisha and Tim, he continued to speak German to them. Tim remembered being overwhelmed in the pope's presence. He was unable to speak, and had tears in his eyes. Finally, Trisha spoke and said, "Oh, Your Holiness, we are Americans." The pope smiled broadly and responded in English, "Oh, wonderful." At the close of his visit, the pope leaned forward, put his arms around both Tim and Trisha at the same time, and said, "I want you two to pray together."

When all individual audiences with the pope were complete, security barricades were taken down so the other pilgrims could walk about freely. A group of people, mostly women, came rushing over to Trisha. They grabbed her hands, kissing them, and stroked her hair. Tim asked a woman nearby, "What's going on?" She said, "We could see the Holy Father having a long conversation with you and hugging both of you. We saw how special you were."

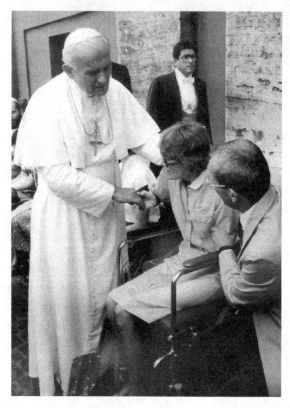

Tim and Mary Patricia Gahan meeting St. Pope John Paul II at the Vatican, summer 1983. "I want you two to pray together."

After the papal audience, Tim and Trisha went to rest and recuperate at the hotel. It had been almost two weeks of tough travel. When they flew back to the United States, my sister Maura met them at the airport. Maura remembered, "At the airport, I saw Tim pushing Trisha in the wheelchair. She had on her lap a gallon-size bottle filled with water from Lourdes. Both of them agreed that it was a trip of a lifetime!" Throughout the trip they felt the hand of God guiding them.

During the next two years, her health continued to decline. Although Trisha struggled physically, she was always in good cheer. She said, "I know there is a purpose for this. We may not understand what that might be, but God has a plan."

The following is a homily on suffering given by Fr. Gahan years later:

Good Friday, "And bowing his head, he handed over his spirit."

Today is the darkest day in the liturgical year. The altar is bare. The liturgy is subdued. All is quiet. At noon today the parish youth reenacted the way of the cross, and tonight we again recall the passion and death of Our Lord. The unimaginable suffering and gruesome death of Christ occupy our thoughts. We try to envision and understand what Jesus endured for our sake. Our attention is first focused on the physical suffering of the Son of God: mutilated flesh, thirst, horrible puncture wounds in the scalp, swarms of insects, deep bruises, contusions and hemorrhages, sweat running into deep lacerations, cramps, gasping for breath, nerves rubbing against iron spikes driven through the hands, the entire body screaming for relief that does not come. There is only wave after wave of excruciating pain. Then we shift our thoughts to the shame of the cross: the humiliation of being publicly lashed, mocked, and stripped of his clothes. But beyond these tortures there is more, much more. In our first reading we were told that Jesus, the suffering servant foretold by the Prophet Isaiah, bore our infirmities and endured our sufferings. He freely took the suffering of all mankind, pain of every description, to himself, and by his stripes we were healed.

When I thought about the suffering of others that he endured, two images came to mind. One was when I was a helicopter machine gunner in Vietnam. One of my first missions was the evacuation of the dead and wounded of a Vietnamese Army battalion that had been in heavy enemy contact for almost two days. I remember landing at their position at first light on a cold, rainy, windy early February morning in 1967. Our first load was of the more urgent cases, and I recall one poor soul lying half curled up on a muddy poncho. Most of his clothing had been cut away, and although he had been given some aid, he was still bleeding from several wounds. He was in obvious pain, shivering, and looked at me with tired, imploring eyes. In the months to come I was to see many other badly wounded and maimed men, but I remember him especially well. Here was a man who was probably not Christian and perhaps never heard of Christ, yet Our Lord took his suffering on himself this day.

The other image is that of my wife. She suffered greatly for many years from a debilitating and painful disease that finally took her life when she was only thirty-five. She was devoted to Christ and his Blessed Mother, and prayed regularly and fervently that her suffering be accepted by Our Lord as prayer for others and their intentions, in reparation for sin, and especially for me and our children. In our second reading, St. Paul wrote that in suffering Jesus became the source of eternal salvation for all who obey him. She understood that well, and that her suffering was bound up in his. This consoled and comforted her, gave her amazing strength, made her love God all the more, and encouraged her to confidently approach the throne of grace to receive mercy and to find grace for timely help. Yes, Good Friday is about suffering: the physical suffering of Christ, the humiliation heaped on him, and Our Lord subsuming our suffering. This day the Savior accepted the pain of suffering humanity. When we look at the crucifix, we should try to see not only Jesus' suffering, but that of our fellow man. God bless you all.

Trisha died on July 28, 1985. She was only thirty-five, and though young, was a true inspiration to all. Terence was twelve years old and Katie was nine when their mother passed away. Over the years, Fr. Gahan donated items in memory of his beloved wife. There is a stained-glass window of the Blessed Mother at St. Michael Catholic Church in Jasper, Texas, and a Station of the Cross (Veronica Wipes the Face of Jesus) at St. Paul the Apostle Church in Spartanburg, South Carolina. He arranged for flowers to be delivered to her grave at Quantico National Cemetery in Virginia on Mother's Day, her birthday, their wedding anniversary, Christmas, and St. Valentine's Day.

Terence shared memories of his mother:

> *In the spring of 1981, I remember my mom and I regularly sitting in the kitchen of our home at Marine Corps Logistics Base in Barstow, California. We were practicing for the Mount St. Joseph second-grade spelling bee. We did this in the evenings after dinner and the dishes were being run in the portable dishwasher. As the dishwasher hummed, we would go over the vocabulary list. After cooking, cleaning, taking us to and from school, and suffering from the effects of MS, she still made the time to work with me in the evenings. Attempting to get me focused must have been very difficult for her as I liked to dance around the kitchen in socks and act like a goofball. Lovingly and patiently, Mom would help me transition to settling in and studying the vocabulary list with her. When we got rolling on the list, we would slip into a sweet academic flow as she would positively teach, encourage, coach, and pull things out of me she knew that I was capable of spelling. After a good study session with mom, I'd feel really like a million bucks, and I knew that we had worked hard toward the goal of competing well in the second-grade spelling bee. Contest day came, and much to the surprise of almost everyone (especially myself), I won! The person that*

was probably not surprised, that knew that I could do this and much more in life, was my mom. She was a dedicated mother, an excellent teacher, and pulled the best out of everyone she came into contact with, and I am certain that is one of the reasons why my dad loved her so much.

During the 1983–1984 school year, our family was living in base housing in Quantico Virginia. One of our family activities at that time was to play board games. A game that we played was called Survive! In the game of Survive! players escaped from an exploding island and moved their Meeples (me + peoples) to safety. There were hazards in the water— sharks, etc.—and players would move their Meeples to safety by boat. Not part of the game but part of my mom's personality was to allow other players' Meeples into her rescue boat. I remember begging my mom to allow my Meeples on the boat, and as she was very nice in all aspects of life, including playing board games, she went along with the idea. This strategy did not get her close to winning the game; and in fact, once my Meeples were in her boat I threw her Meeples out of the boat. Looking a little deeper into this event as it relates to her life, it seems to me that she knew who she was, knew that I was going to throw her Meeples out of the boat, but she was going to do it anyway.

What did I learn from her? First, I learned to never let other people's Meeples into your boat! Actually, the opposite of that is true, and something that I learned from my mom is to regularly place the needs of other people ahead of your own. Both my mom and dad have been outstanding examples of this as they placed their needs second to those of their family, or in dad's case, the Marines or parish he led. In both their unique ways, they have lived life as servant leaders.

Another thing I learned was inspired by my mother, and that is to teach people that can be hard to reach. As a career I have chosen to work with 'at-risk youth' and special needs students for the last twenty years, and I think this can be traced back to some deep-rooted psychological imprint my mom had on me as a child. I am all the better for that as a result, and I hope that most of the children and young adults I've taught would agree."

Katie shared her thoughts:

My mother seemed to balance my father, with his larger-than-life personality that has been described vividly in these pages. She had a calm, kind manner. And although she seemed quieter than my dad, I remember that she had a wonderful sense of humor and laughed all the time. She was utterly compassionate, in big ways and small. She was the best person to challenge to a board game, because she had no competitive streak. She would rather never win a game of checkers again in her life than risk hurting her children's feelings. This attitude did not go both ways, of course, and my brother and I took great joy in our unearned victories.

When we lived in Barstow, California, my mom was very involved in the school that Terence and I attended, Mount Saint Joseph Catholic School. Before I even started kindergarten, she was already a room mother for Terence's class, and would let me tag along to school parties and field trips. I was not too nervous when kindergarten began because I had already spent so much time at the school. She and my dad were dedicated to the school and parish, and played major roles in fundraisers and other activities.

In the days before I started school and when I only went to morning kindergarten, much of the day would be just my mom and me at home. I loved that time with her. We would watch soap operas while folding laundry in the living room. We would work in the kitchen together. I loved cleaning the stove, and she would set me up with a step stool, a rag, and a bottle of Formula 409. We would strip the beds and change the sheets. I would take the bedspreads to the laundry room by putting one end on my head and dragging the rest behind me on the floor. "Look, I'm Princess Diana!" I would say, imagining my Holly Hobby bedspread was the elaborate train from her royal wedding gown. My mom and I loved that wedding dress and the whole spectacle of the royal wedding.

She loved music and encouraged me to play the piano. I was not particularly accomplished, but she was always supportive of my attempts. She had many favorite artists, and as her MS progressed, we often spent time listening to music together. She would ask me to put on her Placido Domingo records, and she would marvel at how long he could hold a single note. My son Milo, now a sophomore in high school, has been singing in the school choir since sixth grade, and I often wish she could have heard him sing. Of course, I wish she could have met all six of her grandchildren. I can see aspects of her in all of them. Bridey is an avid reader, just as my mother was. Mary Patricia got her name and her freckles. Finbar has her height. Although everyone agrees that Conan is a miniature version of his Pappy, he has her sense of humor. Milo has her empathetic nature, and Betsy has her quick wit.

Years after she passed away, I came across some old audio tapes that she had recorded. Back in the days when long-distance phone calls were expensive and

Zoom hadn't been invented yet, she would send tapes of the family to her parents in Dallas to keep in touch. Some included just my mom and dad telling the Hogans of the latest happenings in their lives, some featured the whole family, and at least one was made by my mom when my dad was "in the field" with the Marines while she managed two young children on her own. They are small glimpses into her daily life that tell part of her story. Whether it's my parents describing the new "hi-fi" stereo that they just bought or my mom, Terence, and I excitedly discussing the brand-new movie—Star Wars—we saw in the theater, the tapes capture those stories. It all comes together to show that a life is the collection of these small moments.

That is what this book about my father feels like to me. This is a collection of stories from people who have known him over the course of his life. Some of his moments are roles in large, historic events like the Vietnam conflict; others are smaller, and maybe only involved one other person, but made all the difference in the world to them. I thank my aunt for gathering them, large and small, in this book.

The summer following Trisha's death, my brother took a ten-day vacation to Ireland while the children were at summer camp in New Hampshire. The trip was to combine getting away alone for a while to collect himself after a difficult year with a visit to the Emerald Isle, the land of saints and scholars. He rented a car and had no fixed itinerary. Tim wandered the provinces of Connaught and Munster and visited our grandfather's birth place and the townlands from which Trisha's family had emigrated. It was a refreshing and interesting holiday.

Other trips to Eire followed over the years: a couple of vacations with a brother priest and two with my brothers Teddy and Mike to attend weddings. Our family has retained a strong connection to Ireland. In 2012 our brother Michael and his wife Betsy hosted a family reunion billed as *Siompóisiam Dúchais Éireannaigh* (Irish Heritage Symposium*)* in Boston that focused on family history.

Fr. Gahan and his family wearing Gahan shirts at the dedication of a new Celtic High Cross headstone, donated by my brother Michael and our sister-in-law Betsy, on a family plot in a cemetery near Boston in 2012. From left to right: Fr. Gahan, Terence, Bridey, Conan, Mary Patricia, Kate, Finbar, Leo, Milo, Katie, and Betsy.

Chapter Nine

The Orient, USMC Part III

"These living conditions are somewhat different than I had here twenty years ago as a lance corporal for helicopter machine gunners' school!" Tim exclaimed after arriving at Camp Hansen Okinawa, Japan, in June 1987. Two years after Trisha's death, Lieutenant Colonel Gahan received orders to Camp Hansen, Okinawa, Japan. Arrangements were made for Katie and Terence to live with us in Jasper, Texas, during his deployment.

Tim arrived after a very long flight—four and a half hours from Los Angeles to Oakland to Anchorage, Alaska, and then nine hours to Japan. Lt. Col. Timothy M. Gahan, USMC, was assigned deputy camp commander of Camp Hansen, Okinawa. With over 6,500 troops, it was the largest military installation in the Pacific. His position could be described as deputy mayor of a midsize town. He was involved in many things and was kept plenty busy. A major responsibility was maintaining excellent relations between the Okinawans and the Camp Hansen Marines. His accommodations, a suite of rooms, were most adequate and conveniently located just across the street from the Officers' Mess.

Deputy Camp Commander of Camp Hansen, Okinawa Lt. Col. Timothy M. Gahan, USMC, summer 1987

He began cultivating relationships with the locals. Shortly after arriving at Camp Hansen, Lieutenant Colonel Gahan participated in the Kin-Cho Community Festival, an annual event sponsored by the local Chamber of Commerce. Activities got underway on Saturday afternoon with a parade through downtown Kin-Cho. The camp commander and Tim, as deputy camp commander, joined the mayor, his deputy, and president of the Chamber of Commerce in leading the parade. They stomped along, marching to band music in their "happi coats" made for the occasion, waving to the crowd lining the street. Happi coats are short Japanese kimono robes worn over clothes. Tim remembers a local television station crew covering them as they moved along the mile-and-a-half route to the city fairgrounds. He felt like the grand marshal of the New York City St. Patrick's Day parade. At the fairgrounds he remembers being presented a huge silk flower with streamers to wear on his coat. identifying him as the deputy commander.

Tim wearing a happi coat at Kin-Cho Community Festival, Okinawa, 1987

As Tim described in a letter, "Dignitaries were seated under a canopy directly in front of a covered and well-decorated outdoor stage. This was generously provisioned with much exotic food and drinks—local beer, sake, sushi, etc. The midway behind us was filled with all manner of vendors and merchants. The atmosphere was very festive. One event followed another, either on the stage or near it. The program included a dragon dance, children's choir, concert of traditional music, and culminated with sumo wrestling."

The most popular event was the beauty pageant. As should be expected, hundreds of Marines rushed to the front near the stage as the girls began to come on. Thirty Filipina bar hostesses clad in bathing suits (the very small variety) competed for the Miss

Kin-Cho title. Tim was one of the five judges and described it as "a very tough job, but somebody had to do it!" Events were scheduled until 10:00 p.m., but shortly after 6:00 Tim excused himself to attend a social event at the Camp Hansen mess. A few lieutenants from a battalion due to rotate to Hawaii cooked two 130-pound pigs at a nearby beach and carted them to the club for a pig fest. A full house feasted on the tasty pork while listening to a dance band. It was a grand finale to the first day of the festival.

Another afternoon found Tim back at the fairgrounds celebrating an Obon festival. Obon is a Japanese custom to honor the spirits of one's ancestors. Again, the Marines were treated to some very different kinds of entertainment: more sumo wrestling, a variety show broadcast live to all Okinawa, singing, dancing, and the like. Lieutenant Colonel Gahan was interviewed by a newspaper reporter and he had his picture taken with all the local politicians. The festival closed with an Obon dance. Hundreds of people, Tim included, formed concentric circles around the stage and danced to the music. Tim recalls, "At first I had no idea what I was doing. I quickly spotted a middle-aged woman dressed in a kimono who appeared to know all the intricate movements, and I simply attempted to mimic her actions. I think I was the only American dancing, and I'm sure provided the Okinawan comic entertainment."

On another occasion he attended an Obon dinner at the home of a Japanese family. On arrival, the man of the home escorted him to the home altar where the ashes of his ancestors were kept. Incense sticks burned in front of the urn in the decorated shrine. Tim remembers, "I felt a thousand eyes on me as I made the sign of the cross then prayed privately." Following a wonderful meal and much toasting from small saucers that were said to be over three hundred years old, Tim was asked to deliver a brief speech. He concluded the speech with, "May their souls and all the souls of the faithful departed, through the mercy of God, rest in peace."

The waters around Okinawa are rich with fish. Tim went deep-sea fishing with the camp headquarters staff by charter boat. They departed the Kadena Marina at 7:30 a.m. and dropped anchor near some small offshore islands about an hour west of Okinawa. It was a beautiful day to be on the ocean; warm, clear, with a gentle breeze. There were twenty aboard, and most everyone caught something. Tim caught a deep purple tiger fish that weighed in at something less than a pound, and a pinfish somewhat larger. He caught both using squid as bait in about 100 feet of water. On their return to the boat basin, they stopped for a time and all went swimming. It was a great way to end a most enjoyable excursion. They docked tired and sunburned about 4:30 p.m.

Tim traveled to Camp Mt. Fuji on the island of Honshu in the fall of 1987. Though stationed at Camp Hansen while overseas, the 1st Battalion, 7th Marines had been training at a camp near the base of Mt. Fuji, an extinct volcano. Tim arrived at their camp in the late afternoon and met with the officers and men that evening. The executive officer of the battalion was a close personal friend of Tim's for many years. The following day Tim toured the camp, and that evening he and his friend left to climb the 13,000-foot mountain. They began the ascent at 11:00 p.m. on a cool moonless autumn night. Years later, as an ordained priest, Fr. Gahan gave an Easter Sunday homily remembering this experience.

Easter Sunday, "He is not here, for he has been raised just as he said."

In the name of the Father . . . We started our annual Lenten journey early last month, and this past week we began Holy Week, the holiest and most important time of the church calendar. On Sunday we celebrated the triumphant entry of Our Lord to the holy city of Jerusalem with palm branches held high. On Thursday we remembered Christ's Last Supper with his apostles, when he washed the feet of those who would spread the Good News after his death and resurrection, and instituted the Eucharist that we offer at every Mass— it is the source and summit of our faith. Friday, our attention was on the passion and death of the Son of God. Our altar was stripped, our sacramentals covered in violet cloth, and our tabernacle was open and empty. It was on that day Jesus was beaten, whipped, and crowned with a crown of thorns for the remission of our sins, and suffered the ignominious death of crucifixion for our redemption. Yesterday we mourned his absence. But today we rejoice that Our Savior "has been raised just as he said." God had raised his only begotten Son from the grave!

Some years ago, a good friend and I climbed Mt Fuji, an extinct volcano on the island of Honshu in Japan. It's a climb of almost 13,000 vertical feet. We started our ascent about eleven o'clock on a cool, moonless autumn night, and made good progress through the small hours of the morning. Every hour or two we came across a small hut along the side of the trail that had a campfire in front of it. We stopped at them and braced ourselves with strong, hot green tea and branded our hiking sticks with small branding irons that were kept red hot in the fire. These brands noted the elevation of the way stations and marked our progress on the journey to the top. As we slowly ascended, the air grew thinner and colder, we could feel our muscles tighten and our steps shorten, and the climb got steeper, but we pressed on.

From time to time, we came upon other hikers who seemed completely spent. We encouraged them in a mixture of Gaijin and broken Japanese to persevere in the quest, and most did. We were all pilgrims on the same journey. As the hours passed, we became more tired, the wind blew stronger, the temperature continued to drop, and the trail became more rugged. In places we were forced to climb on our hands and knees, or compelled to use safety lines. The morning twilight found us just below the rim of the volcano, and the knowledge that we had but a few hundred meters remaining renewed our strength.

Finally, we arrived at the summit at the very moment a small sliver of the sun pierced the horizon where the sea met the sky in the east. We stood there on the pinnacle of the mountain—cold, windblown, hungry, dirty, and deliriously happy.

We witnessed the miracle of a new day. We stood in stunned silence and awe as a golden ball of fire slowly climbed out of the ocean. I'm a man of a certain age and have seen the sun come up in places around the world, but never have I seen it in the way I did that morning many years ago. Now I knew, now I understood, why the Japanese revere Mt. Fuji and Japan is rightly known as the Land of the Rising Sun.

My dear faithful, the arduous climb is Lent, the spectacular sunrise on Mt. Fuji is Easter. The toil of reaching the summit is forgotten in the absolute joy of the dawn. As the sun rose in splendor and glory on that day, so the Son of God and Son of Man rose today. We toil here on earth—often life can be difficult, sometimes even cruel. This too is the climb. But if we follow Christ, we also will experience the Resurrection, something far greater than sunrise on the summit of Mt. Fuji or anything else of this world. Keep climbing. I wish you all a grace-filled Eastertide and may Our Risen Lord bless you all abundantly!"

Standing at the summit of the mountain. "I have seen the sun come up in places around the world, but never this way . . . now I understood . . . why the Japanese revere Mt. Fuji and Japan is rightly known as 'the Land of the Rising Sun.'" fall 1987.

After surveying the top of Mt. Fuji and surrounding countryside for an hour or so, they began to make their way down. Their descent was by a different trail from the one they took to the summit. It took about three hours to hike down through the volcanic ash. This side of the mountain was completely barren—no vegetation, water, or even soil. Tim says it reminded him of a moonscape. On returning to the training camp, he took a shower, had a late breakfast, and then settled in for a long midday nap. After no sleep and nine hours of climbing and hiking, he had no trouble sleeping soundly. That night he attended a Saturday night vigil Mass celebrated by an Italian missionary priest. A Salesian nun, also Italian, was with him. She had been in Japan fifty years and spent part of the war in an internment camp. She was a most interesting character and delightful conversationalist.

In October, Lieutenant Colonel Gahan became acting camp commander and officer in charge of the 9th Marine Regiment rear. A large part of the regiment was off the island on a major training exercise. It was a hectic time for Tim as he was at the helm until the rest of the regiment returned. He was in charge of overseeing the operation of the camp and coordinating activities of the much-reduced regimental staff.

Tim commented that the camp commander, Col. Anthony Zinni, was one of the most competent and personable officers he had the great pleasure to serve with. He was held in the highest regard by all. In a letter to us, Tim wrote, "He knows as much or more about leading men and war fighting than anyone. He has remarkable energy and talent. He is the chief reason this tour seems to be passing quickly and has been professionally satisfying. He has a wonderful sense of humor, inspires people, and is passionately committed to country, Corps, and the 9th Marines. We feel fortunate, indeed blessed, to have him as our leader. He is the epitome of a Marine." Colonel Zinni went on to have an impressive career, including being commander of CENTCOM and a special envoy to the Middle East.

During Tim's time there, he decided to have a personal Japanese seal stamp made. They are called "chops" and have the same legal authority as signature in the western world. Chops are registered with the municipal authority and always properly secured. Tim wanted a distinctive and unmistakably Japanese chop, so he commissioned his secretary to develop *kanji* for *Gahan*. *Kanji* is a system of Japanese writing using Chinese characters. At first she explained it was simply impossible, but finally agreed to attempt it. She consulted a number of experts and must have written scores of proposals before they were satisfied *Gahan* in *kanji* had been perfected. Evidently, she did a masterful job, for when people read the impression, they'd grow wide-eyed, seem perplexed, and finally grin and slowly say, "Ga-ann."

During his yearlong deployment to Okinawa, the Gahan children, Terence and Katie, lived with us in Jasper, Texas. During the summer of 1987, both eleven-year-old Katie and fourteen-year-old Terence attended the Catholic summer camps in New Hampshire that their dad, aunts, and uncles had attended in their youth: Camp Fatima for boys and Camp Bernadette for girls. Terence successfully defended his Camp Fatima Marathon title and won the bronze medal in the senior division best athlete competition. Katie won the Model Season Camper award at Camp Bernadette. This award is given for the best camper during the entire eight-week season—easily the most highly prized award of the year.

Since we had five children, the extra two cousins just joined in with the daily excitement. Terence and Katie stayed connected to their father through occasional letters and phone calls. Unlike today, phone access was limited, so the most common communication was letter writing. He mailed a variety of items from the area. One big hit was headbands for the boys, which were the same worn by suicide pilots during World War II. The *kanji* inscription read *Kamikaze*, meaning "divine wind." *Kami* means "god or divine," and *kaze* means wind. The boys loved them and wore the headbands for Halloween that year.

Terence had a fifteenth birthday shortly after arriving in Jasper in August. Terence was on the junior varsity cross-country team, and in his first meet finished eleventh in a field of over fifty runners. He joined Boy Scouts and especially enjoyed camping. He went bird hunting with his uncle Terry and cousin Tommy, and bagged a dove. Later in the season he went deer hunting with his uncle Terry and nailed a good deer! Bringing home the deer, Terence learned how to field dress and skin it, cut it up, and cook it. He also learned nothing tastes better than your own venison.

Katie celebrated her twelfth birthday in Jasper in September. Her dad sent her a glass-encased doll outfitted in many layers of Japanese dress. Katie joined a Girl Scout troop with her cousin Erin, and started taking piano lessons again.

As time passed, Tim made plans for Terence and Katie to visit Okinawa over their Christmas break from December 4 to January 2. They were all excited at the thought of being together again! Tim planned some interesting and educational day trips, and booked an excursion to Hong Kong during Christmas week. After a long flight, Terence and Katie happily greeted their father. The first morning was spent unpacking, getting settled, and touring the camp. In the afternoon Terence wanted to play basketball, of all things, and Katie and her dad took a stroll through Kin-Cho village. After looking about, they stopped at a tea house. The *mama-san* was much taken with Katie. She said, *"Tak-san kow wa-ee"* (very cute). When it was time to go, she was all smiles and refused payment. The next day, after attending a late Mass, they headed north, saw the largest private collection of seashells in the world, and toured Nago, the second largest city in Okinawa.

During the first two weeks, my brother attended to Camp Hansen and the 9th Marine Regiment matters in the morning and the children worked on school assignments. They toured many villages such as Ryukyu Folk Village and Habu (a highly toxic snake) farm. The village is Okinawa's answer to Colonial Williamsburg. It portrays life on the islands in Okinawa's past. On arrival they encountered a large group of Japanese schoolgirls about Terence's age. As they approached, they began whispering to each other and pointing to him. Tim remembers, "The closer we got, the louder the chatter and giggling. Terence turned crimson and beat a hasty exit."

One day the children attended an Okinawan junior high school. On arrival Terence and Katie were immediately surrounded by a sea of curious girls in blue jumper uniforms anxious to welcome them and eager to practice English. After removing their shoes, they were introduced to the principal and faculty. They were surprised to learn that although the school was but a few miles from the camp, no foreign students had ever visited. The children spent the day in English and music classes. They had a wonderful time, learned a great deal, and were featured in a magazine and local newspaper.

On the left, while visiting their dad in Okinawa, Katie and Terence toured the Ryukyu Mura Takoyama Habu Center, a snake farm. On the right, Katie's photo, taken while visiting a grammar school, featured in an Okinawan newspaper.

Katie recalls another moment from the trip: "One day my father took me to a kimono shop in the town near the base. He had arranged to have me fitted for a custom-made kimono. The shop was filled with beautiful, colorful material. There was so much to take in as I was draped, wrapped, and tucked into the traditional garment and accessorized right down to my sandals. I still have the kimono, and it is a reminder of the special experience that my dad planned for us."

They visited numerous castles, shrines, and temples. Since the weather was very pleasant, they took advantage of it by going to the beach less than three miles from the camp. The water was a bit chilly, but they didn't mind and even went waterskiing for an hour. After climbing back in the boat, the captain told them the fourth largest great white shark ever caught in the world was taken exactly where they had been skiing. He even showed a picture of the shark when it was caught only two years earlier.

Tim and the children traveled to Hong Kong and China during Christmas week. On the day of arrival, they took an excursion around the harbor. The following day was one never to be forgotten: a trip to China! They boarded a hydrofoil bound for the mainland, an hour's journey away. First stop was Shekou, Guangdong, where they toured a museum containing some of the world-famous terra-cotta warrior figures that were unearthed in north China. In Guangzhou (formerly Canton), they saw panda bears at the zoo, a banyan pagoda, and toured the octagon-shaped building Sun Yat-Sen Memorial. Stopping for a meal was an adventure, which included a tasty soup of dog meat. They went to a kindergarten in the new economic zone and then north through the countryside, where they saw duck farms and farmers tilling fields with water buffalo dragging wooden plows. In Canton they also went into a shopping frenzy where most everything was unique. Canton was awash with people, crowds everywhere. Streets were a pulsing sea of bicyclists. It was all so exciting, educational, and interesting.

The day before Christmas they went shopping at the Stanley Market in Hong Kong. They spent the day there among the maze of shops and stalls. They toured Kowloon City that evening. The city was ablaze with lights, and Christmas music filled the streets. All the taller buildings had lighted Christmas scenes, some twenty or thirty stories in height with thousands of colored lights. The streets were closed to vehicular traffic, and they thought all one billion Chinese had turned out for this once-a-year event! Everywhere they went they received long stares from throngs of people. On Christmas Day, they attended Mass at Holy Rosary Roman Catholic Church in Hong Kong. It was celebrated in Chinese. Terence felt very conspicuous, his blond head poking up a foot above the entire congregation. They toured a war museum of historic figures that is the equal of any in the world.

The week following their return to Okinawa, they went to the Exposition 75, a World's Fair type park. There they toured an enormous south sea island pavilion, a large Okinawan museum, a reconstructed Okinawan village, and a giant aquarium. The main tanks must have been city blocks in size and contained dozens of varieties of sharks and scores of species of large fishes.

The great Asian adventure came to an end at the beginning of the new year. It was everything they had hoped it would be and more. Five months later they would reunite with their father in the United States.

Terence and Katie were not the only visitors that Tim had during the time he was stationed in Okinawa. His cousin Quentin Walsh and his family visited as well. Quentin recalls, "With Randi and the five kids, we arrived at his office building just as he was exiting the building stoically escorting two equally stoic Japanese officials. We all jumped out of our vehicle, yelling and screaming our arrival at Tim. He was totally mortified at our greeting exuberance as well as the befuddlement of his official guests. I am sure it was one of his most embarrassing military career experiences. Our visit with him on Okinawa, however, is a favorite family memory."

In the spring of 1988, a local election was conducted to determine who would replace the esteemed retiring mayor of Kin-Cho. St. Patrick's Day was not long after election day, and it was decided to combine a reception for the outgoing and incoming mayors with a celebration of St. Patrick's Day, thereby melding the two events. It would be something unique in community relations. It was March 17, 1988. The Okinawan dignitaries had never experienced an Irish-American St. Patrick's Day party like this one! Guests were driven by motor coach to the Officers' Mess, Camp Courtney. Built high on a bluff on the east coast of Okinawa, the club enjoyed a magnificent panoramic view of the Pacific Ocean. It was an ideal venue for the unique event, impressive yet comfortable.

The Okinawan dignitaries included the mayor, vice mayor, members of the Fishermen's Association, Bar Owners Association, Chamber of Commerce, police department, and community leaders from nearby towns, villages, and districts. Attending the event were Marine commanding officers and senior enlisted personnel of the units from Camp Hansen, along with Marine Corps leadership from other locations throughout Okinawa. The ladies were given green carnation corsages and the men boutonnieres. They were listening to Irish music, enjoying typical Irish fare and lively camaraderie. The event program, "A Hundred Thousand Welcomes (*Cead Mile Failte*)," was printed in English and Japanese, and included pictures of the mayors, the story of St. Patrick, songs, prayer to St. Patrick, St. Patrick's Breastplate, and an Irish blessing. The music and festivities continued well into the night. A wonderful rapport was built that day, and was something no one would soon forget. Also, while deployed during that year, Tim traveled to the Philippines and South Korea to participate in and observe training.

Chapter Ten

The Rest of the Story

Terence's memories of his dad

When I think about Okinawa, I think about the many adventures with my dad. We swam in crystal clear Pacific waters, visited ancient castles, saw Japanese bunkers from WWII, went to an exotic botanical garden, attended an Okinawan school for a day, saw historic little Okinawan villages, ate lots of great of Okinawan soup called *yakisoba*, and went to another place that now reminds me of the resort from the television series *Lost*. My dad and I also played plenty of highly competitive games of ping-pong at the USO club on Camp Hansen. As I started to think about competition, I went on to think about the greatest competition I had with my dad.

This story is one that was a little bit after the time my sister Katie and I went to Okinawa. This story takes place in Parris Island, South Carolina, around the fall of 1988. My sister Katie and I had moved back from our school year in Jasper, Texas, and we were now living with my dad. We lived in the officers' quarters on Parris Island. The house was white with black trim, close to the Beaufort River and the 4th Recruit Training Battalion barracks, which is where female recruits become Marines.

At this time, I was a sophomore in high school attending Beaufort Academy in nearby Beaufort. I was on the cross-country team for the school, doing well and winning races. I was also taller than my dad by this time. I remember thinking something like, "Yeah, I am taller than him," and "I am winning all these races," and "Yeah, I am going to be on the varsity basketball team this year," and "Yeah, I am a man! I am definitely a man!" And you know what I said to myself? "Yeah, I can take this guy." In my head I thought today was going to be the day I was going to "take" my dad in a wrestling match.

Froggy, the word for this type of feeling I had about "taking" somebody is called feeling froggy. That frogginess or itch to prove myself and take my dad was about to be answered.

I was definitely feeling froggy, and thinking in my mind that this old man (who was forty-three at the time and I am forty-eight as I write) was going down today. This was going to be historic! This was going to be the day that the Jukester—another nickname for my dad and slang for someone that is awesome at everything, as well as particularly clever—was going down! In my mind I was going to displace the Jukester and become the new Jukester. It was going to be epic. I knew that I could get this guy. He was going to go down! Big time!

It was a weekend and the weather was nice. We were outside moving between doing yard work of trimming the bushes and mowing and attempting to fix up the Fiat in the driveway. The Fiat was a 1978 red convertible sports car, 124 Spider, he had recently bought and frequently required work. Our biggest success with the mechanic work on the Spider was installing a toy car horn that played "Dixie."

I had decided this competition was going to be a wrestling match, because as a "man" I thought wrestling would be the way to go. I did not want to knock him out with my newfound man strength. So there we were outside, me feeling like a man, and this was going to be the day I was going to "take" my dad in a wrestling match. Prior to the match I needed to intimidate him with trash talking and posturing and letting him know how this man (me) was going to be the new number one Gahan in the house. I am not sure what I said, but I knew it was clever, because after all, I was a man.

I do recall his response though. He said, "If you're feeling froggy, jump!" Well, I was feeling froggy all right, and I was going to jump him. Having decided on wrestling because it is manly, I decided that I was going to run straight at him and overpower my dad with my manhood.

The time for trash talk was over, and now was the time for manliness! I was about thirty feet away from my dad and started to run as fast as I could, straight at him. Yeah, I was going straight at this dude, and he was soon going to be in a world of hurt. Old man! No way! There can be only one! I am going to be the Highlander and the new Jukester!

In my mind I was like Flash Gordon, and because of my pure speed and manliness, something was definitely going to happen to him. To him, not me, no way is something going to happen to me. My legs felt like they were moving like a windmill in a hurricane, and I had extra legs like a windmill has arms; so to complement the awesome leg action I had going, I decided to move my arms like windmills. Going to windmill this old dude today!

And because of the awesome speed I knew I had going, I needed to make some noise as well. So I let out a war cry, "Ahhhhhh!" And I knew he had to be psyched out by this point. This was going to be the moment.

A funny thing happened though. The Jukester did not move as I approached. My dazzling speed, the just-invented impromptu double-windmill technique, and the war cry had zero impact. He just seemed to bend his knees maybe, just a little bit. I was offended that he did not run away from this man, and now he was not going to get it easy with the flailing arms, he was going to get straight arms. Straight arms, Dad, straight arms and hands coming at you! Beware!

Feeling that victory was imminent, in the bag, I began contemplating how awesome it was going to be being the *numero uno*. In hindsight, I should have come up with a real plan ahead of time, or maybe reconsidered this juvenile idea, or paid attention to what he was doing with his slight bend of the knees. Maybe attacking a seasoned, salty Marine was not such a good idea.

Engagement. Then it happened, the moment of truth had arrived. I was now right in front of him, charging hard. The next few moments were both slow and fast at the same time. With knees bent and hands up, the "old man" sprang into action. I don't know where my arms went, but I do know where his landed. The Master's hands (yes, another nickname for my dad is the Master, and he is also known as the "Mogul Master" when we hit the ski slopes) were just inside my shoulders and gripping tightly on to my shirt. I felt like I had come to a full stop, and I kind of did, because the speed and energy that had come from me (amazing man energy) was now entirely transferred to him as he began to roll backward. Back, back he went, and as he went back the bent knees of the Jukester turned into legs that were firmly planted in my chest. My momentum had stopped, and my man energy was now returned to me as it moved me up, up, up into the air and over and side to side, all at the same time. The Master had launched some type of judo roll against me! Except that it was really not the Master who had done this to me, it was me, the man that had created the conditions necessary for the Master to carry out the maneuver. As I was twisted, turned, and flopped in the air by my dad, I was gaining a better appreciation of why he really was the Jukester, the Master, or sometimes "Jukes" for short.

Into the bushes. What goes up must come down. After my flight on this sunny South Carolina Lowcountry day, I landed in the bushes. Into those bushes I went with my long, skinny arms and flamingo legs all askew. In defeat, I lay in the bushes. This was a complete victory for he who would later be named Pappy and Fr. Gahan, and a resounding defeat for me, "the man" and the would-be Highlander. No, today was not going to be the day that the Jukester was going down. In fact, the competition between my dad and myself was really not a competition at all.

Out of the bushes. As a caring father, my dad wanted to make sure that I was okay, and I was. I was fine. The only thing that hurt was my pride. So immediately after being Jiu-Jitsued by him, my dad helped me get out of the bushes. The Jukester brushed off the leaves that had stuck to me on the crash landing. He made sure I was well. All was well. He gave me a helping hand, started making light of the situation, cracked jokes about what just happened, and helped me laugh about the asininity of the situation. To this day, it is something we still joke about, and it makes for a good story to tell and retell, and to sometimes embellish.

Nephew and niece stories

When our son Ted was ten years old, he had a school assignment to write about "My Favorite Relative." "Uncle Tim is a lieutenant colonel officer in the Marines. Uncle Tim's life must be really neat. He is a man who drives around a lot and does wild things, so I guess you could say he's a 'Wild Man.' He has blue eyes, brown hair (there's not much of it), and he's a tall man with a deep voice. If he wants someone, even if they aren't far away, he yells for them. He has one daughter that is twelve and one son that is about eighteen (he's so tall it seems like he can reach the clouds). His son and daughter are very nice. I really do think he is my favorite relative."

Our son Brian has fond memories of his uncle Tim. "Uncle Tim was always a cool uncle. When I was ten, he came to visit us in our small East Texas town. He drove up the driveway around 9:00 p.m. in a rented red convertible and honked the horn. After we all ran out to greet him with big hug, he said, 'Jump in the car, I am taking you all to the Dairy Queen for a banana split.' We all had our pajamas on, but we jumped in the convertible and off we went, riding around town in a convertible in our pajamas, eating banana splits. It doesn't get much cooler than that!"

Uncle Tim made memories at a family reunion memory for our youngest son, Michael. "During a family reunion, we were all swimming in a hotel pool. We were having fun with water games when Uncle Tim came over to the sideline of the pool and announced in a booming voice, 'All right, everyone out of the pool. Let's go!' We quickly scrambled out of the pool, along with all the hotel quests who were also using the pool. When Uncle Tim speaks, EVERONE listens!"

When my sister Madonna's daughter Brigid had an "older friend" writing project in high school, she immediately thought of her uncle Tim. "Once gunning down North Vietnamese and later in life 'Saving Souls' as an aspiring diocesan priest. Yep. that's my uncle Timothy Gahan. As you can see, this man had a very diverse life starting from day one! As he looks back through the years, he has had a 'Good run!' and would change very little if he were to do it again. As my uncle likes to say in Irish: *Slan agus beannachtai De leat!* Or, 'Goodbye and God's blessings to you!'"

Chapter Eleven

The Corps, Part IV

On returning from Asia during the summer of 1988, Tim reported to the Marine Corps Recruit Depot, Parris Island, South Carolina, where he was assigned as the G-4A (assistant logistics officer). They lived close to a marina, bought a boat, and enjoyed the Lowcountry life. During their stay, Terence, a sophomore at Beaufort Academy, won the South Carolina State Cross-Country Championship. Katie, an eighth-grader, took first prize in a competition in a statewide Latin forum.

While stationed at Parris Island, Tim hosted a Gahan clan reunion. Although the Gahan siblings were scattered from Massachusetts to Texas, Florida to Ohio, we always remained a close family, with a reunion every few years. A Marine Corps base was an especially exciting and unique place to host a reunion. In USMC fashion, Tim had a list of activities with times, events, locations, remarks, and points of contact listed. We all checked in on June 15, 1989, meeting at Tim's quarters. In front of the quarters, tied between two trees, was a huge vinyl banner in Kelly green letters, "Gahan Family Reunion" superimposed on a shamrock. We greeted each other and enjoyed happy and lively conversation while enjoying a summer buffet. Our mother, known as Nanny, was smiling from ear to ear.

The following day began with the presentation of Morning Colors, during which our mother was recognized, followed by a recruit graduation parade. It was a mild summer morning, and it was impressive to see all the proud Marines and their family members who traveled from states east of the Mississippi. The parade was the culmination of three months of arduous training. Later that morning we toured the base, which included a private tour of the commanding general's quarters by the general's wife. Noon Mass was followed by a river cruise, waterskiing, and rappelling. Our young son Tom remembered being surprised at the height of the rappel tower. "It was so high and scary, and I could hear Uncle Tim cheering us all on as I and all my cousins each took turns rappelling." That night we dined at the marina with a catered Lowcountry supper of traditional Frogmore stew, local blackened fish, shrimp, gumbo, sausage, oysters, and corn on the cob.

A Gahan family reunion tradition includes the "Gahan Follies," where each family displays their talent or lack thereof. The eight families sometimes sang a song, recited a poem, told jokes, or even performed a skit. My daughter Erin remembered, "The three Gahan uncles of the family always brought much laughter and fun at reunions. Uncle Tim always had a loud voice and laugh."

On Saturday we toured the beautiful and charming city of Beaufort and included more waterskiing in the afternoon. Some opted to play volleyball or golf. We ended the day with a Mass at the Blessed Sacrament Chapel offered for our departed relatives. After Mass each grandchild shared a memory of their grandfather, Col. T. P. Gahan, who had passed away eleven years earlier. The final event of the reunion was dinner at the Officers' Club, after which family photos were taken. Our mother loved the reunion, and having it on a Marine Corps base made it quite special.

Not long after reporting to Parris Island, Tim received notice to attend the Naval War College at Newport, Rhode Island, the following summer. The Naval War College develops strategic and operational military leaders. Katie and Terence attended Bishop

Connolly High School in nearby Fall River, Massachusetts. Terence continued to develop as a track and cross-country runner. He won the 1989 Fall River High School Cross-Country Championship and was named to the all-Southeastern Massachusetts Cross-Country Team (First Team). Katie was an accomplished runner in her own right. She was on the freshman girls' cross-country team at the beginning of the season, and finished the year on the varsity squad.

Being a student at the Naval War College in Newport, Rhode Island, Tim enjoyed being near family and friends. Our brother Michael and sister Maura, as well as many other relatives, lived in the Boston area. Most Marine bases are in the South with mild climates, so being in New England was something different, even experiencing a real winter.

After graduating from the Naval War College, my brother was transferred to Camp Lejeune, North Carolina, where he was assigned as the assistant operations and training officer of the 2nd Marine Division. In August 1990, Operation Desert Shield began the buildup of coalition forces led by the United States to drive the Iraqi Army out of Kuwait. Desert Shield became Desert Storm when air operations began on January 17, 1991. The ground offensive began February 24, 1991, and is known as the "100 Hour Ground War."

While Tim was at the Naval War College, the wife of a friend who was on staff at the school approached him to consider having Terence and Katie stay with their family should Tim be deployed with the 2nd Marine Division. His friend's family knew and went to school with Terence and Katie. After Christmas 1990, the children lived with his friend's family in Rhode Island and returned to Bishop Connolly High School. It was Terence's senior year. He had attended four different high schools during his high school years, and was now finishing up back at Bishop Connolly High School.

Lieutenant Colonel Gahan was to join the 2nd Marine Division in Saudi Arabia in January 1991, but before leaving his orders were modified, redirecting him to join Battalion Landing Team 3/8 at the Naval Station in Rota, Spain, in February. The purpose of the reassignment was for him to become familiar with BLT 3/8 in preparation for assuming command of the unit the following month.

On March 15, 1991, Tim assumed command of BLT 3/8, the ground combat element of the 26th Marine Expeditionary Unit (Special Operations Capable). The day after the change of command, he spoke with all the NCOs and then staff NCOs in the morning, and that afternoon he held an officers call at the Officers' Mess at 1500. Exactly at 1500 he asked the adjutant, "What time on deck?" The adjutant answered, "Fifteen hundred, sir." Tim, the new BLT commander said, "Secure the hatch!" That was it. You were either there or you weren't there. There were a few officers missing. You could hear a pin drop. Years later, a combat engineer who was present remembers, "In the Marines, we call the time when you start your attack the line of departure or LOD. When LOD was set at a particular time, everybody was in coordination for the attack. Lieutenant Colonel Gahan started off the afternoon comments in a jolly but firm way. He stated, 'Gentlemen, gentlemen, I want to be clear. When we say we cross the LOD at 1500, we cross the LOD at 1500.' When I think of him that story is exemplary of his simultaneous firmness yet compassion. In retrospect, things are clear. I see that with Colonel Gahan. He didn't harp on it, but it was powerful. And no one was ever late again. We got the message."

Many in the battalion had just returned from a six-month deployment and would soon be going out again for another six months, so Lieutenant Colonel Gahan tried to leave weekends free for the men to spend time with family or enjoy a bit of liberty. Occasionally they had to work straight through the weekend; however, he tried to stay away from training on Saturdays and Sundays. On several Friday afternoons, Lieutenant Colonel Gahan invited the subordinate unit commanders to get together at his quarters in a relaxed environment, giving an opportunity for the group to talk about things in common and BLT policies. A young first lieutenant recalled, "He had us all over to his quarters. I thought that was great to reach out to us. As leaders, we are told to be familiar but not friendly with our subordinates. So I thought it was great to have a little bit of social time."

Lieutenant Colonel Gahan believed in leadership by "walking around" to develop a feel for things. For example, later while training at Camp de Canjuers in the French Alps, he and the sergeant major showed up before first light one morning at a rain-soaked campsite. They surprised the combat engineers bivouacked there and asked the Marine on radio watch where they might get a cup of coffee. There was no particular reason for the visit. He was there to get a sense of things with the troops.

In June 1991, Tim deployed to the Mediterranean with the 26th Marine Expeditionary Unit (26th MEU). This unit was an air-ground task force with about 2,400 personnel consisting of four major components: a command element, a ground combat element, an aviation combat element, and a logistical support element. Tim was part of the ground combat element, Battalion Landing Team (BLT) 3/8, which mustered 1,247 personnel and was spread across four ships—the USS *Wasp*, the USS *El Paso*, USS *Sumter*, and USS *Ponce*. Tim and the BLT command element were billeted aboard the USS *Wasp* (LHD 1).

At 40,500 tons displacement, the USS *Wasp* was larger than World War II aircraft carriers. It was designed for fast troop movement over the beach, and to accommodate a full range of helicopters, conventional landing craft, amphibious vehicles, and vertical/short takeoff and landing (V/STOL) jets, which provide close air support to the assault force. The ship cast off from Morehead City, North Carolina, on its maiden voyage to the Mediterranean in June. After clearing the Straits of Gibraltar, the first stop was Fiumicino, Italy. The US ambassador to Italy requested the 26th MEU to make a port call to celebrate Independence Day. The Marines obliged, displaying equipment, weapons, vehicles, and air combat element jump jets and helicopters. A contingent of Marine officers was on the embassy grounds for the celebration of the Fourth of July.

From Fiumicino, the 26th MEU steamed to Iskenderun, Turkey and then flew to Sirsenk in northern Iraq (Kurdistan) via Turkey. They went into Iraq to replace the MEU that was located near the city of Zakhu and scheduled to return to North Carolina. The airstrip at Sirsenk was originally built to facilitate travel to Saddam Hussein's nearby mountaintop palace.

A "no fly" zone with a ceasefire was in effect, and there had been no fighting for some time. Tim's battalion was to familiarize themselves with the terrain, environment, and Iraqi and Coalition Forces positions so that in the event Marines needed to be reintroduced to the area they would be familiar with it. Part of the air support for 26th MEU was provided by an army Blackhawk helicopter squadron just across the Turkish border to the north. Tim recalled, "It was the only time I have been on a Blackhawk helicopter. We took recon flights over Iraqi Army positions. We saw defensive and artillery positions with the Iraqi crews, but there was no activity. They weren't shooting and we weren't shooting. It was an odd sensation."

Northern Iraq July 1991. At right with Kurdish children near Zakhu. The bridge in the background was built by the Romans over 2,000 years ago and still in use.

The Amphibious Ready Group then sailed to Haifa, Israel. The battalion debarked for training at Camp Adam and Camp Shivta. Camp Shivta is in a remote region, which facilitated desert training and crew-served weapons firing. A crew-served weapon is a weapon system that requires a crew of two or more individuals performing tasks to run at maximum efficiency. While in Israel, he stopped at Jerusalem and briefly prayed at the Wailing Wall.

Then on to Cap Serrat, Tunisia, where the 26th MEU trained with Tunisian Special Forces. It was force-on-force training, where one element played the role of offense and the other defense. Cap Serrat was picturesque, situated on a bay with beautiful beaches, and the weather was fair. One day while on reconnaissance, Tim noticed on his map an area indicating Roman ruins. He and two others traveling with him stopped at the site and noticed a well nearby. The men enjoyed the water, drinking and washing the grit and grime off their faces. While there, they observed a young Tunisian girl. She was staring at the Marines from a distance. Little did Tim know that decades later, the encounter with this girl would work into a homily based on the narrative of Jesus meeting a Samaritan woman at the well.

The gospel reading of the Samaritan woman at the well reminded me of a minor incident that took place almost thirty years ago. I was serving in a Marine infantry battalion conducting training in Tunisia during the summer of 1991. While on reconnaissance in a dry, remote, sparsely populated area we came upon a well. It was not the kind of cistern well described in the gospel narrative but one that had a hand pump; otherwise, the scene was almost identical. The well looked very much out of place in that arid landscape. In any event, we stopped to wash our sweaty, dust caked, sunburned faces; refresh ourselves and refill our canteens.

Seemingly out of nowhere a young woman carrying a large blue plastic pail appeared about fifteen yards from us but seemed reluctant to come any closer. She was clothed from her head to her sandals, studied us intently for a time, and then slowly came toward us. I greeted her in Arabic but she only stared at me. I called out to her in French but she said nothing in reply. Then after a long pause and in a halting voice, she said in French we were welcome to the water. Almost immediately a man in the distance shouted something to her and she hurried off. We finished cleaning up and then left all the rations we could spare at the well in a gesture of goodwill.

In thinking about the incident later, I concluded the girl could have remained away from us until we departed, but was curious about us and defied the strict cultural rule to have nothing to do with infidels, especially foreign men and heavily armed nonbelievers at that.

I think the Samaritan woman in our gospel reading must have experienced something like that Tunisian teenage girl. It's likely the Samaritan woman asked herself: "Who is this man? Why is he speaking to me? Why am I interested in him? Why am I breaking a strict social convention to satisfy my curiosity?" She must have been astounded that Jesus, a total stranger, knew all about her. In any event, by speaking to the Samaritan woman Our Lord demonstrated he was not bound by any cultural, religious, political, or social barriers. His message of salvation was universal. The Kingdom of God was for all, not just the Chosen People.

By replying to Jesus when he asked her for a drink, the woman was responding to the action of grace in her soul; it was the first stage in her change of heart. After Our Lord's grace had penetrated the intimacy of her conscience, she made an act of faith: "I can see you are a prophet." Her faith was rewarded by Jesus revealing himself to her as the Messiah, the one called the Christ. Moreover, this conversion did not stop with her acknowledgment that the Jewish man she met at the well was the Christ, the living water; drinking the water that Jesus gives makes someone extraordinary. Once she accepted him, she told others about him and, "Many of the Samaritans of that town began to believe in him." So how does this concern us? Well, our journey should be one of ongoing conversion, cooperation with others so that we will never thirst and will become "a spring of water welling up to eternal life."

Memories like that would be integrated into many homilies in his future. But giving homilies and being a Catholic priest were far from his mind at this time.

On the left, woman at the well in a dry remote area in Tunisia who, speaking in halting French, offered the Marines water. On the right, Lt. Col. Timothy M. Gahan, USMC, in Tunisia, summer 1991.

From Cap Surrat, the Marines made port calls at Palma de Mallorca, Balearic Islands, off the coast of Spain; Benidorm on the Spanish coast; and Sousse, Tunisia, depending on which ship they sailed. Tim, being aboard the USS *Wasp*, went to Palma, well known for its beautiful beaches and festive nightlife. "Cinderella" curfew was in effect, having to be back on the ship by midnight. Everyone had to have a liberty partner for safety and to make sure you were back aboard the ship on time. Midnight was not a popular time to be back on the ship as dinner onshore began around 9:00 p.m. and the club scene didn't really start until midnight. The USS *Wasp* was tied up along a pier and open for tours. While in port, the ship's captain hosted receptions and dinners for a number of distinguished guests. These included Spanish royalty (Princess Maria and Don Juan, Count of Barcelona) and King Constantine and Queen Anna of Greece.

After the refreshing liberty break, it was on to Toulon, France, and then to Camp de Canjuers, a training area in the foothills of the French Alps. In a nearby village there were a large number of retired French Foreign Legionnaires. The legionnaires challenged the

Marines to a soccer match, and of course the Marines were up for it. A day or two later, a group of Marines went to the village to play the retired legionnaires. Keep in mind that the retired legionnaires were still in good shape, fairly young (in their forties), and soccer was their favorite sport.

News of the early evening match spread quickly among the villagers, and the sideline of the field was set with tables of food and wine, making it quite the event. Everyone in town showed up. The Americans were beaten badly but had a fabulous time. The Marine team coach, a lieutenant, said, "OK, we played your game, how about if we come back another night and play one of our sports?" The villagers readily agreed, though they had no idea what kind of game it might be. So a softball game was arranged for another night. After about the second inning everyone could see the French didn't understand the rules of the American game well. The game was stopped and new teams were organized of part Marine and part legionnaire players. There were even more villagers from the surrounding area attending this game than the soccer match, and even more tables loaded with food and wine. It was an international summer sporting event not to be forgotten.

While the sergeant major and Lieutenant Colonel Gahan were driving through the village of Draguignan, France, they noticed a sign that read "American Cemetery" and decided to investigate it. The Rhone American Cemetery was well kept and quite lovely. They walked about and read the headstones of the Americans killed in southern France during WWII, displaying the date they were killed and their unit. Eight hundred fifty-eight Americans are buried there. Those interred died mostly in the summer of 1944 during Operation Dragoon, the Allied invasion of southern France from the Mediterranean. The headstones are arranged in straight lines, divided into four plots, and grouped around an oval pool. Small gardens are placed at each end of the cemetery. After the war, families were given the opportunity to disinter their loved ones to fly them back to the US, while others opted to leave them buried there with their comrades.

Deployments are not without risk. It seems that during every deployment there is at least one death. Tim remembered, "We lost a young corporal, Corporal Boddie, while at Camp de Canjuers. He developed a respiratory problem in the mountains in France. We sent him back to the ship for medical care. However, he died a couple of days later." Corporal Boddie, twenty-two years old, was a native of St. Croix, Virgin Islands, and was assigned to Company L, 3rd Battalion, 8th Marines. He was survived by a wife and a young son. There was a memorial service for him onboard the USS *WASP* conducted by the BLT chaplain.

Cpl Regan Boddie, USMC, died of a respiratory problem on September 17, 1991. He was twenty-two years old and survived by a wife and son.

Following the training of the 26th MEU in France, the Amphibious Ready Group got underway for Antalya Bay, Turkey, to participate in a large naval exercise in the eastern Mediterranean. Operation Display Determination '91 included ships from the United States, Italy, Turkey, United Kingdom, Spain, and France. Training can sometimes be dangerous. The following year, during Operation Display Determination '92, two missiles fired from the USS *Saratoga* struck a Turkish destroyer, resulting in loss of life as well as extensive damage to the ship.

At the conclusion of operations with allied navies, the USS *Wasp*, USS *Sumter*, USS *El Paso,* and USS *Ponce* got underway for Saros Bay, Turkey. There the 26th MEU conducted an amphibious landing and participated in a large exercise with the Turkish Naval Infantry

Brigade (Turkish Marines). The area of operation was near where the Allied Powers conducted an unsuccessful attempt to control the sea route from Europe to Russia during World War I, known as the Dardanelles Campaign. They did force-on-force training with the American and Turkish Marines on one side and the Turkish Army on the other, in which they took turns being on the offense and defense. At the conclusion of the exercise there were military skills competitions that included marksmanship competition and a five-mile run. The Turks then hosted a dinner party of traditional Turkish food and included belly dancers for entertainment.

Next the USS *Wasp* made port at Rhodes, Greece. It is the largest of the Greek Islands and is famous for one of the Seven Wonders of the Ancient World, the Colossus of Rhodes. The Colossus of Rhodes was a statue of the Greek sun god Helios. It stood approximately 108 feet high, about as tall as the Statue of Liberty. It collapsed during the earthquake of 226 BC.

Interestingly, BLT 3/8 had a Marine who was fluent in many languages. He spoke Turkish, Arabic, Hebrew, Italian, Spanish, and French, as well as English. Wherever he went he could speak the language, except when they arrived in Greece. When they docked in Rhodes, the first thing the Marine did was go to a newsstand where he could buy a Greek phrase book/dictionary. He certainly had a gift for languages, which served him well on this deployment. Once while Lieutenant Colonel Gahan was touring the troop berthing area, he saw another Marine reading a book in his bunk. Interested, Gahan asked him, "What are you reading?" The Marine showed him the book. It was written in Hungarian, but the Marine was American born and had no Hungarian ancestry! It was a keen interest in a Hungarian girl that had prompted him to learn the language.

After leaving Rhodes, the 26th MEU sailed for Crete and then on to Valencia, Spain. After a port call there, the USS *Wasp* then sailed to Almería, Spain, where the embarked Marines unloaded to train with the Spanish Legion at nearby Camp Sotomayor. While there, a Marine pilot, Capt. Thomas Driscoll, twenty-six years old, was killed in a Harrier jet accident. The USS *Wasp* had (V/STOL) vertical and/or short takeoff and landing jets known as Harrier jets, able to take off vertically or on short runways. When his AV-8B Harrier jet was in trouble, Driscoll steered away from the Spanish village of Villagarcia de la Torre and ejected with the plane upside down. The investigation determined that a problem with the ailerons caused the crash. He was survived by his parents, siblings, and fiancée. His father, John Driscoll, said that his son showed an interest in flight at an early age, and built more than fifty model airplanes, which remain boxed in his parents' attic. "We don't have the heart or stomach to throw them away," his father said.

The evening after the crash, a memorial service was held in the field during evening formation. Just before the start of the service, with the sun going down, the X Bandera (10th Battalion) of the Spanish Foreign Legion came marching up with their traditional quickstep, wearing their distinctive *chapiri* caps with red hanging tassels and piping to join the formation. The BLT 3/8 chaplain, a Catholic priest, read holy scripture and led all in prayer. The simple service, conducted on the open plain at Camp Sotomayor, was as impressive as any ever held in the grandest of cathedrals. Lieutenant Colonel Gahan wrote a letter to the family in which he described the moving tribute.

On the left, Capt. Thomas Driscoll, USMC, twenty-six years old, was killed November 11, 1991, in a Harrier jet accident. When his plane was in trouble, Driscoll steered away from a Spanish village and ejected with the plane upside down. On the right, my brother (back row, sixth from the right) with Spanish Foreign Legionnaires at Camp Sotomayor near Almería, Spain.

The next stop for the USS *Wasp* was Barcelona, Spain—the vibrant, beautiful, and historic capital of Catalonia. Preparations were being made for the 1992 Olympic Games hosted by the city, and construction of venues for sporting events was well underway.

The final port call of the deployment was Rota, Spain, site of a large base used as the turnover point for units coming to and leaving the Mediterranean. En route to North Carolina, BLT 3/8 was delayed briefly off the coast of the Dominican Republic due to unrest in the area; however, they were able to make it home for Christmas. The Battalion Landing Team was disbanded shortly after returning to Camp Lejeune.

In March 1992, Tim was reassigned as the commanding officer of Headquarters Battalion, 2nd Division. There were about 1,500 Marines and sailors in the unit. It was organized into companies that provided service and support to the division, which included a military police company, small-craft boat company, communications company, motor transport company, and the division band. His family lived in base quarters. By this time, Terence was a freshman at New Mexico State University and Katie was a junior in high school.

In the summer of 1993, Tim transferred to Quantico, Virginia, where he was assigned as vice president of the Marine Corps University. The Marine Corps University is the collection of Marine Corps schools and educational programs: Communication Officer Career Course, Sergeant Major Academy, the Marine Corps War College, Basic School, Officer Candidate School, Amphibious Warfare School (now Expeditionary Warfare School), War Fighting School, and various educational programs.

After nearly three decades in the Marine Corps, Colonel Gahan began to consider retirement. He had already been given a colonel's command in the Fleet Marine Force, and not expected to return to the operating forces. At forty-nine years old, the rigors of Marine life were becoming more challenging. As time progressed, it became clearer that retirement was in his near future. He retired on November 1, 1994, ready for a new challenge to do interesting and worthwhile things in another chapter in his life. Once a Marine, always a Marine!

Pvt. Terence H. Gahan, USMC, with his father Col. Timothy M. Gahan, USMC (Ret), May 1995. Colonel Gahan assisting his daughter Katie out of the limousine at her wedding, June 2000.

Chapter Twelve

Priestly Vocation

"It might surprise you to learn the first person who asked me to consider becoming a priest was my mother-in-law!" Fr. Gahan liked to say. When folks heard that, they would do a double take. Tim recalls that his journey to the Roman Catholic priesthood was different from most.

On November 1, 1994, on the Feast Day of All Saints, Col. Timothy Mannix Gahan officially retired from active duty in the US Marine Corps. Mass was celebrated that day at the U.S. Marine Memorial Chapel in Quantico, Virginia. Tim paused at the chapel doors. His mind traveled back nine years. The funeral for his precious wife, Trisha, was held in this very chapel. Not much had changed—same altar, same stained-glass windows. Now it would be the beginning of a new chapter of his life. After Mass there was a retirement ceremony that included a bagpiper and a breakfast reception at the USMC Research Center.

My brother had a Marine Corps friend who retired a year earlier, and was the principal of a Catholic high school in Scranton, Pennsylvania. They had served together in the 2nd

Division at Camp Lejeune. Both were attracted to Mass in the Extraordinary Form (Latin Mass). He informed Tim that the Priestly Fraternity of St. Peter had recently established a North American Headquarters in the Scranton area, and encouraged him to consider a position on the staff. The Priestly Fraternity of St. Peter, founded in 1988 in Germany, is a religious community that offers the Mass exclusively in the Extraordinary Form. In 1991, they began apostolates in two dioceses in the United States, one in Dallas and the other in Rapid City, South Dakota. Tim was intrigued, so he traveled to Elmhurst, Pennsylvania, and spoke with the superior, Fr. Arnaud Devillers, FSSP. Two weeks later they had another conversation and he offered Tim the position of business manager of the North American District.

My brother recalls, "I was with them until 2001 and the work went very well. I was convinced it would be successful as there was a genuine need and the timing was right. If the Blessed Mother wants this for her Son, it will happen, no matter what. It was exciting work and gratifying to watch the community flourish. What a great blessing to have been a part of it."

In 2001, Col. Timothy M. Gahan, USMC (Ret.), was named the recipient of the Fidelis Award, an award presented once a year in recognition of services to the fraternity in enabling it to pursue pastoral and liturgical work in the service of the church. By this time, Colonel Gahan had served seven years as the North American District business manager and was deeply involved in the fraternity's intensive search to locate and acquire a ready-built home or build a new facility for its growing number of seminarians.

After serving the fraternity for many years, it seemed to be an opportune time for Tim to write another chapter of his life. Fr. Paul Carr, FSSP, the district superior, said, "The colonel was here at headquarters almost from the beginning. Both his vibrant personality and the special contribution that he brought to his work will be sorely missed." Through his work with the fraternity board of advisors, Tim met James Wilson, who founded the J.E. Wilson Advisors, LLC, the oldest fee-only financial planning firm in South Carolina, located in Columbia. Working closely together on financial planning with the board of advisors, Tim and James got to know each other well. As a consequence, James offered Tim the position of business administrator of the firm. Tim thought it would be an interesting and new challenge in an area with a moderate climate, and he accepted.

As my brother was packing to relocate to Columbia in 2001, he took a small statue off the bureau in his bedroom. In his hands Tim held a travel-worn four-inch statue of St. Sebastian. He carefully wrapped it, preparing to ship it across country to the McFall family and remembered first seeing the statue fifty years earlier. The statue was given to the family about 1956. At the time, one of our Walsh cousins was attending St. Sebastian School in a Boston suburb. The statue was thought to have been an auction item at a school fundraising event. My three brothers kept the statue on a chest of drawers in the bedroom they shared. It always had a prominent place in our home.

St. Sebastian was shown as a strong warrior holding a sword and shield. Due to the statue's small size, it was able to travel the world. The statue stayed with Fr. Gahan during his 1991 deployment to the Mediterranean on the USS *WASP*. It traveled with him to Italy, Turkey, Iraq, Israel, Tunisia, Spain, France, and Greece. It traveled with his family during moves to Hawaii, Rhode Island, Texas, California, Virginia, North Carolina, and South Carolina. It also accompanied Colonel Gahan to Okinawa and Thailand. If only that statue could talk, what stories it could tell!

I remember receiving a package marked "fragile" from my brother and had no idea what it was. When I opened it and saw the worn statue, I immediately remembered it in our home growing up. We placed the statue in a place of prominence in the four McFall boys' bedroom. It held a special meaning to Ted, who took the name Sebastian for his confirmation name. Later, when Ted moved out on his own, the statue went with him. Years later, Ted gave one of his sons the middle name Sebastian. Ted's wife, Dorothy, commented, "The statue has gone through a lot and is missing part of his sword and some of his shield. He looks like a true warrior!"

This St. Sebastian statue traveled the world with Colonel Gahan, including his 1991 deployment to the Mediterranean on the USS *WASP*. If only this statue could talk, what stories it could tell!

St. Sebastian was born into nobility and joined the Roman Imperial Army and became an officer. He ministered to persecuted Christians and spent much of his time converting prisoners of the Roman Army. He was a gifted healer, using the sign of the cross and converting fellow soldiers. He was eventually caught and martyred for his faith. When he was found to be a Christian, Emperor Diocletian ordered him to be killed by arrows. His body was pierced with arrows, and he was left for dead. He recovered and once again sentenced to death, and was beaten to death with clubs in 288 AD. He is the patron saint of archers, athletes (for his energetic evangelization), and dying people. He is typically represented bound to a tree and wounded with arrows. He is buried along the Appian Way in Rome. One of the seven pilgrim churches of Rome was built over his relics and burial site. St. Sebastian was an incredible healer, evangelist, and model Christian soldier. His feast day is January 20. *St. Sebastian, pray for us.*

While living in Columbia, Tim taught religious education at the local parish and joined the St. Columba Division of the Ancient Order of Hibernians, an Irish Catholic fraternal organization. Later, he became the two-time state chaplain of the group. Tim would periodically ask himself, "What am I called to do?" In praying about it over time, it occurred to him that there might be a possibility of a vocation to the priesthood. He would often ask, "Lord, how do you want me to serve you?" He prayed frequently to the Blessed Mother, asking her to help him with discerning the call to become a priest.

Years later, Fr. Gahan gave a homily about discerning one's vocation.

Vocations Sunday

> *Today we celebrate the fourth Sunday of Easter and World Day of Prayer for Vocations. The word "vocation" comes from the Latin "voco," "vocare," meaning to call, and our Catechism defines it as "The calling or destiny we have in this life and hereafter." It goes on to say that "God has created the human person to love and serve him; the fulfillment of this vocation is eternal happiness. The vocation of the laity consists in seeking the Kingdom of God by engaging in temporal affairs and directing them according to God's will. Priestly and religious vocations are dedicated to the service of the Church as the universal sacrament of salvation." Most of us think of a vocation as a calling from God reserved exclusively to the religious life. The truth is we all have a vocation. By our common baptism, Christ calls us to serve him and our fellow man. A vocation is not a career choice . . . it's a way of life . . . that pleases God and brings us closer to him. It moves us to use our talents for the greater honor and glory of God, and to the benefit of our brothers and sisters. It brings us real comfort and genuine happiness in the knowledge we are doing his will and assisting*

others in the attainment of the salvation of their immortal souls. Calls to the priesthood, permanent deaconate, or professed religious life are vocations of a particular kind.

Of course, not all are called to these vocations, but all are called to participate in promoting them, especially the priesthood. The most efficacious way of doing this is prayer: prayers of supplication, of petition, that many will answer the call to be a priest, deacon, sister or brother, and that those who answer this call will be good and holy servants of God and his people.

This is the aim of World Day of Prayer for Vocations. In addition to prayers for an increase in these callings, especially here in the Diocese of Charleston where the need is so very great, there are other things that all can do to promote vocations. To my mind, one of the most powerful is to simply ask someone you think might have a vocation to seriously consider serving God as a priest, deacon, sister or brother.

At the beginning of our formation for the priesthood, my brother seminarians and I went on a weeklong retreat. I remember that during one of the retreat conferences we were asked to explain to the group how we came to a decision to pursue a vocation to the priesthood. There were as many different stories as there were members of the group, but without exception they all included something like, "a friend said I should be a priest," or "someone I admired and trusted asked me 'Did you ever think of becoming a priest?'" Or "someone who knew me well told me she was praying that if it was God's will I should become a priest." (I think it was the fellow's former girlfriend, and she might have just been trying to get rid of him!) Or some other such thing. In every case, something someone said forced us to examine a call to the altar.

In my case it was my mother-in-law. Some of you might be considering a vocation to the religious life, especially the priesthood. To you, I say two things: first, don't dismiss the notion because you do not think you are worthy of it. Get over it. No one is worthy to be a priest. And second, remember the words of Pope John Paul the Great: "Be not afraid!" Lastly, let us all pray fervently and without ceasing that Our Lord will send many laborers to work in his vineyard.

Tim recalls, "At that time there were a couple of people who mentioned a vocation to me. I don't think anybody takes it on himself. Someone saying 'I think you would be a good priest' gets you thinking that maybe I could be a priest one day, and compels you to think and pray about it. When people say something like that, it can stay with you. Honestly it became a real bother to me. I thought the only way I can get this worked out is for me to apply and see how it plays out. I didn't think I would be accepted by the diocese for a lot of reasons. Foremost was age (I was fifty-seven), and that I was not well known in Columbia. However, everything just started falling into place. In the late fall of 2002, James and I were discussing plans for the next year. I told him I wouldn't be there next summer and I thought we needed to do a search for someone to replace me." Tim was quite satisfied with his position, so James asked why. Tim responded, "I'm seriously thinking about pursuing a vocation to the priesthood." James was surprised, and stated, "For any other reason except being a priest, I would try to dissuade you. I can't argue against that. I get it."

Tim recalled, "The children didn't know I was discerning a priestly vocation. In 2002, both children were married, and we were at Folly Beach for Christmas. One night, I said, 'Christmas is a time for surprises and I have a surprise for you. I am leaving the firm this summer, and we'll go around and you tell me what you think I am doing next.'"

Katie recalls, "My husband, Leo, was sure he had some terrible disease, and my first thought was that he was going to become a priest. I'm not sure if I said it out loud right away, since it seemed somewhat far-fetched, but it was the first thing that popped into my head."

Tim remembers, "Terence was the last one to guess. He said, 'I think you are going to study to become a priest.' The thing I remember about it is Katie turned her head toward me and almost under her breath, but loud enough for me to hear, said, 'I was going to say that, it was the first thing that came to mind.' I don't know how this is going to play out. I've begun the process—psychological testing, physical exam, interviews, references, transcripts, and background investigation. I have to do a lot of things— meet with the vocations board and bishop, etc.—all in fixed sequence, and any one of those things could rule me out."

Katie said, "It was very much like my father to turn his announcement into a game and make us all guess. We were all surprised, excited, and very proud of him. Leo likes to say that on paper he has the most intimidating sounding father-in-law possible: a retired Marine Corps colonel *and* a Roman Catholic priest!"

Before Trisha's father, George H. Hogan, died in 2000, he mentioned to family members that he was praying that Tim would become a priest. After Trisha died, Tim would periodically visit her parents in Dallas for a few days. On one visit after Mr. Hogan died, he traveled with Mrs. Hogan to the "Irish Ridge" of Kaufman County, Texas. During the visit she told him, "Tim, George and I thought you would be a good priest." Tim replied, "Oh come on, Grandma!" My sister Sheila remembers, "One Christmas I received a Christmas card from Helen Hogan (Trisha's mother). She mentioned how wonderful it was that Timmy was going into the seminary. What? That was news to us! I questioned my siblings but they knew nothing of it. I asked Timmy about it and he said that perhaps Mrs. Hogan was getting up in years and could have been a little confused. Later he admitted that Mrs. Hogan was not confused, and he threw his mother-in-law 'under the bus' on that issue. He had not shared the info with us until he was sure that he was accepted by the Diocese of Charleston to go to the seminary. What a life-changing step this would be! He told us that he felt he might be called to the priesthood, and that it may or may not work out but at the end of his life he didn't want to have any regrets about not giving the seminary a try. Of course, it did work out!" *"Not my will, but yours be done"* (Lk. 22:42).

My sister Sheila continued, "Several years ago I met a high school classmate of Tim and Ted's in El Paso. He remembered our brothers well and asked if Ted was a priest, as that was the path Ted was thinking of after high school. When I said no, but that Tim was the priest, he was so surprised! (Ted and Tim were born just short of a year apart—Irish twins.) Ted was the more reserved and quiet personality and Timmy was the jokester. Out of the eight of us, Timmy was the most energetic and outgoing, so no wonder their former classmate was amazed that it was Tim that God had chosen to become a priest."

Even though Tim's high school classmate was surprised, those of us in the Gahan family were not. We came from a very loving home where faith and family were taken seriously. Our parents were staunch Roman Catholics who made sure their children knew their prayers, attended Mass, received the sacraments faithfully, and were educated in the faith, both by word and example. They prayed constantly for their children. Conversations around the dinner table provided an environment that encouraged all of us to live out our God-given vocations. My father died in 1978, and my mother in 1995, so neither saw their son ordained a priest. However, we know and feel their presence daily and see the fruits of their labor.

Helen Hogan, Tim's mother-in-law, died in January 2004 and did not see him ordained to the priesthood. However, at Thanksgiving 2003, Tim went to Dallas to see Grandma. She knew he was in the seminary, and she saw him wearing a Roman collar.

Chapter Thirteen

Seminary and Ordination

"*You did not choose me; I chose you and appointed you to go and bear much fruit, the kind of fruit that endures*" (Jn. 15:16). How else can one explain a widower, father, retired Marine Corps colonel, not only becoming a priest but celebrating his first Mass on July 28, 2007, the anniversary of the death of his precious wife, Trisha?

Col. Timothy M. Gahan, USMC (Ret.), entered Blessed John XXIII National Seminary in Weston, Massachusetts, a suburb of Boston in 2003. Tim recalled, "It was a cold start academically for many of us. We were college graduates, many had graduate degrees or professional credentials, but it had been quite some time since most of us had been in a classroom."

The mission of Blessed John XXIII National Seminary (now Pope St. John XXIII National Seminary) is to form older men for the priesthood, or what is known as "delayed vocations" or "second career vocations." The age range is from thirty-five to seventy, and are from varied backgrounds. Tim began formation to the priesthood at fifty-eight. In his class of twenty, three were older than him. Each man had his own vocation story of listening to God's call to the priesthood.

Tim made many good friends in the seminary. There were about seventy seminarians in the student body from dioceses throughout the United States, primarily from east of the Mississippi River. It was a four-year program of formation. He recalls, "Everyone was supportive of one another. There was little attrition, as you might expect. At that age, the men had been thinking and praying about their vocation for a good while."

The seminary program is based on four pillars of formation: human, spiritual, academic, and pastoral dimensions. Human formation assists in developing leadership skills. Spiritual formation's goal is to help each seminarian become a priest after the mind and heart of Christ. Each is assigned a spiritual director to assist the seminarian in their ongoing discernment of a priestly vocation. Pastoral formation includes academic coursework and internship in pastoral studies. Academic formation or intellectual formation assists candidates in attaining competencies and skills necessary for ministry. Surprisingly, one thing Tim remembers in particular is the quality of the food at the seminary. "It sure was good, and not just good for institutional food. It really was good!"

During his seminary years, Tim completed a liturgical Spanish course in which he was taught basic prayers in Spanish. Between his first and second year, Tim audited an introductory Spanish course at the University of South Carolina in Columbia, and did the same the following summer at Coastal Carolina University in Conway when he had an assignment at the parish in North Myrtle Beach. Tim volunteered to serve as lector when the Mass was offered in Spanish every few weeks. Tim would practice the readings in Spanish before Mass, writing notes and hints of the correct pronunciation of words to assist him.

Everyone at the seminary had a house job or jobs. Tim's job was maître d' or head waiter at festive dinners on solemnities and special feast days. Tim would organize the wait staff, table set up, and dinner service. A local barber gave the seminarians haircuts before passing away suddenly in the summer of 2003. Since there was a barber shop at the seminary, Tim started giving haircuts to his brother seminarians, just as he did on the troop transport ship to Vietnam thirty-seven years earlier. His barber skills came in handy yet again! Another house job Tim had was raising and lowering the flag every day. Along with the American flag, he also raised different flags on special occasions, such as the Vatican flag, Marine Corps flag, and Irish Tricolor. He even arranged for the local fire department to use a bucket truck to place new lines on the flagpole.

Can you imagine a baseball team named "the Relics" made up of men between the ages of thirty-five to sixty, playing their hearts out and beating a much younger group of men? Well, that is just what happened when a softball game was arranged with St. John Seminary, the diocesan seminary for Boston. Tim was the manager/coach of the team. Our brother Michael sponsored the team and provided shirts, hats, and team pictures. The game was played during Tim's third year. He remembers, "We absolutely crushed the youngsters. We were very well organized and had practiced. The day of the game, our team, the Relics, showed up in uniform, warming up on the field, surprising the opposing team. We won the trophy! The following year, my last year, St. John's team came ready to play, and they beat us soundly."

While at seminary, everyone knew he was a retired United States Marine colonel. He was recognized quickly by his swagger, demeanor, haircut, and commanding voice—everything about him screamed Marine! Some of the faculty were worried that he might come across as a little strong to parishioners. He is also remembered as being very proper, very much a gentleman. Once while in the refectory (dining room) enjoying lunch, a fellow seminarian spilled something on his pants. The seminarian muttered, "Oh, I'm going to have to wash my pants now." Tim replied, "Only women wear pants, men wear trousers." After going on for some time on this issue, the other seminarian said, "This is all coming from a man who for thirty years wore a blouse and scarf." (That is what Marines call them.) Tim, embarrassed, turned beet red and said, "It wasn't a scarf, it was a field scarf."

Tim returned to South Carolina during the summers to do pastoral work at different parishes. It involved a variety of things such as visiting homebound parishioners, property maintenance, training altar servers, and assisting with vacation Bible school. The first summer he was assigned to Good Shepherd Catholic Church in Columbia. The next summer, he served at Our Lady Star of the Sea Parish in North Myrtle Beach. The third year, as a transitional deacon, he was assigned to Church of St. Mary, Our Lady of Ransom in Georgetown.

My brother has long had a special devotion to St. Peter, Apostle. He took the name Peter when he received the Sacrament of Confirmation. Curiously, he was tasked to deliver the homily at Blessed John XXIII National Seminary on the Feast of the Chair of St. Peter, 22 February, during his final year of formation for the priesthood. It was the only time he was asked to do so. The homily or sermon was usually given by the celebrant. A deacon would deliver the homily perhaps once a month. In any event, speaking to all the faculty and his brother seminarians, he described St. Peter as a man with whom it was quite easy to identify in many ways, and the example of someone to emulate. In writing about my brother's life, it became plain to me why he has such a strong connection to that fisherman from Galilee.

> *Mt. 16:13–19, St. Peter, "And so I say to you, you are Peter, and upon this rock I will build my Church." The Basilica of St. Peter in the Vatican is at the center of the Catholic world . . . indeed all Christianity. Around the copula that rings the high altar in this magnificent structure are inscribed in Latin the words from this morning's gospel:* Tu es Petrus *(you are Peter), and upon this rock I will build my Church and the gates of the netherworld shall not prevail against it." These are the words of institution of the Church established by God made Man . . . the Church He entrusted to the simple fisherman from Galilee. Not surprisingly, the* cathedra Petri, *the chair of St. Peter can be found at the basilica named in his honor. It is located above the apsidal altar in a gigantic casing of bronze by Bernini. There is little reason to doubt St. Peter, foremost of the apostles, presided from the chair. And until the fourteenth century newly elected popes were solemnly*

enthroned on it. Of course, the chair is far more than a simple piece of ancient wooden furniture; it is the symbol of the authority of the papacy. Ubi Petrus, ibi Ecclesia: *where there is Peter, there is the Church.*

In this morning's gospel, Peter "gets it." To the question put to him by the Master, "Who do you say I am?" he replied, "You are Christ, the Son of the living God." Jesus responded by declaring him blessed, the only individual disciple he called blessed, and told him he will be given the keys of the kingdom and the power to bind and loose. But Peter didn't always "get it." It was he who sliced off the ear of the servant of the high priest in the garden of Gethsemane; who denied his Lord three times; who resisted having Jesus wash his feet at the Last Supper; balked when Jesus told him to cast his nets; could not keep Christ company for an hour when needed; sank into the sea when his faith waned and begged his Master to save him from drowning; was nowhere to be found as Our Lord hung on the cross; pleaded with Jesus to "depart from me, Lord, for I am a sinful man," and only two verses later in this gospel was told by the Savior to "get behind me, Satan! You are a hindrance to me; for you are not on the side of God but men."

Why recount the misdeeds and foibles of the great saint we honor today? Because he is the example, par excellence, of faith, hope, repentance, fortitude, and perseverance, and we would do well to emulate St. Peter. Perhaps in his shortcomings we can see some of Peter in ourselves. Maybe we connect by sharing some of the same difficulties, frustrations, and deficiencies. His example of seeking forgiveness and ongoing attempts at amendment of life should both inspire and console us.

Peter is an eminently likeable personality. Many are attracted to this man, who often appeared to get in his own way. Many years ago, when my son and I were discussing his impending Confirmation, he asked to take the name Peter. When I asked him why, he said, "Dad, I think I understand St. Peter better than most all the other saints. I mess up now and again, and so did he, but he was always sorry and never gave up. He really loved Christ. I pray to St. Peter when things don't go right. I think he understands. I think he 'gets it' and helps me." I thought that was good reasoning for a fourteen-year-old lad, and agreed his name should be Peter.

St. Peter, pray for us.

In 2007, the Diocese of Charleston was blessed to have seven seminarians ordained to the priesthood. A search of diocesan records revealed that it was the largest ordination class in the history of the diocese, which was established in 1820. Bishop Baker referred to the soon-to-be priests as the "Magnificent Seven." One man was ordained early in the year and six other men were ordained during the summer. To accommodate the expected crowd of family, friends, and supporters, the diocese held the ordination in the Convention Center in Columbia rather than the cathedral in Charleston.

Diocese of Charleston priestly ordination, July 27, 2007. Fr. Timothy Gahan is at the far left.

Typically, ordinations take place in early June. In 2007 however, it was celebrated on July 27. It was all in God's plan, because the next day was the anniversary of Trisha's death, when Tim celebrated his first Mass. More than eighty family members and out-of-town friends from Wyoming, Washington, Virginia, Florida, Texas, Massachusetts, and other states attended, as well as many local friends. These included his son Terence and his wife Kate and their children Bridey, Mary Pat, and Finbar; his daughter Katie and her husband Leo and their son Milo; all his seven siblings and their spouses; numerous cousins, nephews, and nieces; Trisha's sister Eileen; and Marine Corps friends, some of whom he had not seen in many years. It was a glorious, blessed event. "It is an unusual experience to have your father go through the process of seminary and becoming a priest, but I can't think of anyone better to do it," Katie said. "His relationship with God is something everyone can aspire to. It's incredible. He has a good understanding of people, having been in the military and working in different areas. He can relate to people of all different backgrounds."

Tim, now Fr. Timothy M. Gahan, offered his first Mass at St. Joseph Catholic Church in Columbia. The recessional hymn was the "Marines' Hymn," complete with a bagpiper. The reception following Mass consisted of a Lowcountry boil of typical South Carolina food, which included shrimp, sausage, potatoes, and Frogmore stew. Fr. Gahan gave the traditional blessing of a newly ordained priest to the attendees. His five sisters—Sheila, Maura, Heidi, Madonna, and I—sang a song to him. "If you knew Timmy like we know Timmy, oh, oh, oh, what a guy!" It was a joyous afternoon!

Gahan sisters singing at the ordination reception. "If you knew Timmy like we know Timmy, oh, oh, oh what a guy!"

Newly ordained priest blessing one of his five sisters. On the right, Fr. Gahan with his immediate family at his ordination.

"It's wonderful to have a father who's a priest," Terence said that day. "My father is a man of great faith, and this just follows the way he's lived his life. He raised us right—we went to Mass all the time, and he would do the readings and pray with us at dinner. This is the fulfillment of a long process." Katie shared, "My mother died when I was nine. Now that I am a parent, I don't know how my dad did everything for us. He was an incredible father. I hope that I can be as committed to my son and any other children I may have. Keeping God and church involved in everything you do. It's not just about going to church on Sunday. God is always there and is always listening."

Chapter Fourteen

New Parish Church

Following his ordination, Fr. Gahan's first assignment was as parochial vicar at St. Joseph parish and school in Columbia, South Carolina. Life as a parish priest was a new role for Fr. Gahan, and one in which he was happy and well suited. He served at St. Joseph Parish until January 2008 when he was transferred to St. Andrew Parish in Myrtle Beach, where he was assigned as administrator pro tempore. Four months later, he became the parochial vicar.

The parish is on the King's Highway and only a block from the beach. Fr. Gahan capitalized on the location, and many days he enjoyed a brief early evening swim. The parish was a second parish for many annual vacationers and tourists. He especially enjoyed interacting with the parish youth. There was quite an active women's organization that sponsored a summer fashion show that featured a surprise guest model in 2009—none other than Fr. Gahan in tie, sharp sports coat, and snappy slacks rather than the black cassock he always wore! When he appeared in the show, all the ladies in attendance were laughing, cheering, and clapping. It brought the house down!

During his assignment at the parish, he was installed as a member of the Equestrian Order of the Knights of the Holy Sepulchre of Jerusalem, a Catholic order of knighthood with the primary mission to "support the Christian presence in the Holy Land." Installation took place in Charleston at the Southeastern Lieutenancy Convention in 2009.

In November 2009, he was reassigned to St. Paul the Apostle parish and school in Spartanburg. The parish had a beautiful church built in 1882 and expanded in 1932, but was far too small to accommodate the ever-increasing number of parishioners. Daily Mass was offered in the church; however, most weekend Masses were offered in the gymnasium. By the mid-1990s, the decision had been made to construct a larger church. Many committees were formed and meetings conducted to plan and raise funds for the construction of the new church. Fr. Gahan remembers the construction company being first rate, and those on the new church committee a joy to work with. The chairperson of the new church building committee was Catherine Welchel, and the steering group consisted of Christopher Crowley, Joseph Lauer, and Father Gahan. The aim was to combine traditional architecture and functionality in the church.

Everyone in the parish eagerly contributed to the successful completion of the Lombard Romanesque-style church. A parish school eighth-grader, Jake Armstrong, came up with an idea for a unique fundraiser. He designed a Lego structure based on the drawing of the new church and asked for a $1 donation for each guess for the total number of Lego pieces in the model. (There were a total of 1,600 colored plastic Lego bricks.) Fr. Gahan asked Jake to announce the winner of the Lego model church contest during the groundbreaking ceremony, where Jake sat on the dais with the other dignitaries participating in the program. Fr. Gahan convinced Jake that when it came his turn to stand in front of hundreds of people to announce the Lego contest winner, he should announce it this way, "And the winner is . . . Fr. Gahan!" Jake is a "by the book" kind of guy, so some didn't think he would do it. But he did. Fr. Gahan played right along as if he were the winner, holding his clasped hands over his head and pumping his fists into the air. What fun! Jake was pleased his joke was taken so well by his beloved priest and fellow parishioners. Afterward, the real winner was announced. When the ceremonial groundbreaking took place, Jake was one of those who used a golden shovel for the ceremony. The Lego model is now in a display cabinet near the east side church door.

St. Paul the Apostle Catholic School student Jake Armstrong designed a Lego structure based on the drawing of the new church on the left. On the right, Blessing of the Cornerstone at St. Paul the Apostle Catholic Church in Spartanburg, South Carolina. Etched in the cornerstone of the church *AD MAJOREM DEI GLORIAM* (To the Greater Glory of God), April 2013.

The groundbreaking was later described in the church dedication program:

> *Our Lady of the Miraculous Medal. "Unless the Lord builds the house, those who build labor in vain" (Ps. 127).*
>
> *Recognizing that it was Our Lord who was to build our new house, in October of 2010 we began a weekly novena to Our Lady of the Miraculous Medal asking Our Blessed Mother to help us in the challenging undertaking to build the new church. Every Tuesday evening since then we have prayed to her to*

intercede with her Divine Son on our behalf. At the groundbreaking on 2 May 2012, Bishop Guglielmone blessed and buried a miraculous medal under the site of the Altar of Sacrifice. Once construction began, blessed miraculous medals were incorporated to the church. Throughout construction they were mixed into concrete, deposited in the masonry blocks, used in the mortar mix, hidden in the walls and roof, and buried in the grounds. Workmen who expressed an interest in the miraculous medal were provided one with a silver chain. Our Lady never fails us and she has favored us in this work to the greater glory of God. We will continue to pray the weekly novena to Our Lady of the Miraculous Medal to ask her continued assistance and thank her for helping us in this unique project. Blessed Mother of God, pray for us.

Chris Crowley recalls, "As members of the steering group for the construction of the new parish church, Joe Lauer, Fr. Gahan, and I met often and got to know each other very well." Fr. Gahan recalls, "We were the executive agent for this project. Our approach was to coordinate all the efforts of those who were involved in the construction. Many were involved: the new church building committee chaired by Catherine Welchel, the City of Spartanburg, the general contractor, and the diocese. It was certainly a collaborative effort."

Their approach was for it to be a "generational church," a term coined by Joe Lauer. Some things would be done by the next generation and more still by the generations thereafter. For example, the frames for the nave windows were made to accommodate heavier glass than was installed so they could later be refit for stained glass. The sacristy was very simple, but in time it would be outfitted with proper vestment cabinets and storage cabinets for liturgical items, and an altar rail would be installed at a later date. The money raised to build the church was put into the bricks and mortar; generations to come will make their mark on it by interior enhancements.

Chris Crowley was responsible for most all of the artwork and embellishments. The stone tympanum (artwork over the front door) depicting St. Paul the Apostle being struck off his horse was designed by Chris. Catherine Welchel coordinated the many activities of the working groups of the New Church Committee in impressive fashion. Joe Lauer made invaluable contributions in both design and construction. He was directly responsible for saving millions of dollars on the daunting project and building the church on time. The names of these three are on the marble dedication plaque in the narthex in recognition of their indispensable contributions to making the dream of a new parish church a reality.

When it was time for the massive ridge beam of the church to be raised, the children of the parish signed their name on it. They were excited and proud to see the enormous beam bearing their name hoisted into place. At the front of the church are three statues: St. Peter, St. Paul the Apostle, and the Blessed Mother. The Blessed Mother statue is centered at the apex of the facade. The statue was hoisted into place on a beautiful fall day while the children of the parish school sang Marian hymns and recited the rosary.

Chris remembers, "After one meeting with our steering group, I made my usual trek up to the church to check on progress. As I walked into the church, I passed a workman that I knew well, who was installing a door to one of the confessionals. As I walked by, he asked me, 'Chris, will you ever use this room?' He knew what it was. In answering, I replied jokingly, 'I would but I don't think Fr. Gahan has that kind of time!' referring to my rather long list of sins. Suddenly, a voice from behind quips, 'Don't worry about it, Chris, I'll pack a lunch!' I didn't know Fr. Gahan was right behind me! We all had a great laugh."

The work continued uninterrupted for a year and a half. Countless obstacles were overcome, unexpected developments straightened out, and problems solved. But eventually it all came together in magnificent fashion.

From the Rite of Dedication program:

The new church for St. Paul the Apostle Parish is dedicated AD MAJOREM DEI GLORIAM *(To*

The Greater Glory of God). This phrase, etched on the cornerstone of the church laid on 5 April 2013, is the cornerstone sentiment of our community of faith. It expressed the idea that any work that is not evil, even one that would normally be considered inconsequential to the spiritual life, can be spiritually meritorious if performed in order to please God. We pray God will be pleased to accept the new church, the fruit of our long labor, as an offering to His greater honor and glory and bless our humble work. We give Him thanks for blessing our efforts to erect a new church in which to celebrate the Sacraments, most especially the Holy Sacrifice of the Mass.

December 9, 2013, the Solemnity of the Immaculate Conception, was a cold, drizzling, rainy day in Spartanburg, but there was excitement in the humid air. The Solemnity of the Immaculate Conception is celebrated on December 8. However, in 2013 it was transferred to December 9 so as not to conflict with the second Sunday of Advent. After years of prayer, great sacrifice, nearly twenty years of planning, and just plain hard work, the church was a reality. The new church seats 820, but on the evening of the church dedication there was an overflow crowd in attendance.

Gahan family and friends from around the United States arrived for the church dedication days before the event. Many travelers filled the historic bed and breakfast inn across the street from the church, where we gathered for buffets and refreshments before and after the dedication. Fr. Gahan's children and grandchildren, along with all the Gahan siblings, many cousins, and nieces and nephews, attended. It was a family reunion. We visited Cowpens Battlefield, the Biltmore Estate in Ashville, North Carolina, and were hosted by a parish family at their home for dinner, at which parishioners enjoyed hearing about "Timmy" growing up! Some US Marine Corps brothers of Fr. Gahan were also in attendance, including Col. Noel Douglas and his wife Brenda from the US Marine Leadership Department. Capt. Gerry Lear, who was a helicopter pilot in Vietnam, and his wife Kathlynn were also there. As someone who served with Tim in Vietnam, Captain Lear had a direct connection with Fr. Gahan, then Lance Corporal Gahan in 1967.

The first-class relic to be sealed in the altar of the church during the Mass of dedication was a piece of a bone of St. Peregrine Laziosi, patron saint of cancer patients. St. Peregrine, born in 1260 in Italy, was an ordained priest with the Servite order. He was cured of cancer after receiving a vision of Christ on the cross reaching out his hand to touch his impaired limb. St. Peregrine was canonized in 1726. Just before the beginning of the Mass of dedication offered by Most Rev. Bishop Guglielmone, the bishop of the Diocese of Charleston, he blessed Kathlynn Lear—who was in cancer remission—with the relic and implored the intercession of St. Peregrine to keep her in good health. The relic was then placed in a custom-made reliquary box made of 300-year-old barn wood, and embedded in the altar.

The rite of dedication included the blessing and sprinkling of holy water, installing the relic of St. Peregrine Laziosi, prayers of dedication, anointing with sacred chrism of the altar and the walls of the church, incensation, and lighting of altar candles. Twenty-five priests attended, including our cousin Fr. E. Corbett Walsh, SJ, a Jesuit from Boston. In addition, there were representatives from other faith communities from throughout the Spartanburg area. Catherine Welchel, chairperson of the new church committee, stated, "Honestly, I'm almost overwhelmed. I am speechless. To be able to build a sanctuary like this to worship our Lord is awesome."

St. Paul the Apostle Church dedicated December 9, 2013, the Solemnity of the Immaculate Conception. After years of prayer, great sacrifice, nearly twenty years of planning, and just plain hard work, the church was a reality.

After the church dedication, there was a champagne/dessert reception in the parish center. Entertainment was provided by the Gahan family. We sang a song to our brother Fr. Gahan and the parishioners, a version of "Rise and Shine and Give God the Glory, People of St. Paul!" It was a festive time, including a skit with Fr. Gahan and his two brothers wearing hard hats building a "church" with cardboard boxes.

A parishioner remembers, "Watching Fr. Gahan build the physical church at the same time building the church (the people) was such a special experience. Brick by brick we watched the structure go up. We attended the groundbreaking, and watched miraculous medals being placed in the holy ground. I can still smell the incense and visualize the beauty of our new church! I had tears in my eyes when I received the Eucharist on the first Mass in our new church. I know Fr. Gahan sacrificed so much to give us this precious gift of a big beautiful house of worship. One thing comes to mind was his dedication. His old silver Honda CR-V seemed to be always present at the church. It is unbelievable how one priest could be in so many places and accomplish so much in a short time. God had a mission to build that church, and using Fr. Gahan's Marine leadership and finance background, he was uniquely able to complete the mission. I know that he entrusted all his efforts to God and the Blessed Mother. He knelt many hours every Tuesday during the benediction and novena, and I am sure many other times too!" One parishioner stated, "Fr. Gahan got our beautiful new church built after parishioners had spent nineteen years of Sundays worshiping in the gymnasium. Oorah! We are so grateful to Fr. Gahan for all he did to complete the new building."

Another parishioner recalled, "First and foremost, Fr. Gahan is 'all in.' They must teach that in the Marines. He is engaged and is engaging. Whether you are one-on-one or in a large group with Fr. Gahan, somehow he can make you feel as though you are central to him. We've heard it said about him and have said it ourselves, 'He poured himself out for us.' He truly does. In his parish, the people truly are the church. He built our church up and he got our new church building constructed—on schedule and on budget. He is the shepherd who cares for his flock, at all times with prayer, and many times with humor. I was never in his office that he didn't give me a blessing before I left. And I always left feeling uplifted."

An employee of St. Paul the Apostle parish recalled, "With Fr. Gahan we received a blessing from God himself. Not only is he an officer and gentleman, but a priest with a pastor's heart who loves people. It wasn't long before the church fell in love with him. Fr. Gahan has a way about him that is contagious, and his sense of humor is second to none. His laugh is like no other. My first impression of him was I felt like I knew him before he showed up. I read his biography prior to his arrival and immediately thought to myself, "I'm going to love him. He knows what it means to have God, family, and country."

A parishioner remembered, "Though Fr. Gahan's lighter side shone through often, he is all business for Mass. He celebrates Mass with the same precision that a watch keeps time. Or as a Marine runs a platoon. Everyone knows their role and when and how to do it. The altar is no place for anything but worship, the liturgy of the

Word and Eucharist. This is where Fr. Timothy Mannix Gahan is at his best and where he seems most at home."

Another parishioner who assisted Fr. Gahan at Mass stated, "I am always amazed at his expression when he elevates the chalice!" The Eucharistic consecration is the pinnacle of the Mass. Many, even lifelong Catholics, have stated that Fr. Gahan has taught them many things about the Mass, thus increasing their knowledge, appreciation, and joy while at Mass."

Offering Mass at St. Paul the Apostle Parish Church, Spartanburg, South Carolina

"Fr. Gahan's homilies were succinct and thought provoking. Just as you would expect from a Marine, Mass always started and ended on time, and would never be canceled. My husband and I would discuss and ponder his messages throughout the week. He often tied in the readings to the catechism of the Catholic church, and you would want to pay attention or you might miss a funny quip that had everyone in church laughing. His way was firm yet gentle, as a loving father. He did not mince words, and some of his homilies were challenging. But because we all knew and loved him, I believe there were many conversions of hearts. During the years he was our pastor, our marriage grew stronger as a couple and we became involved in many parish organizations that we still enjoy."

The "Altar Server Corps" was a very important service for Fr. Gahan. He instituted three levels of altar boys from server, who wore a white surplice; to senior server, who wore a white surplice with black bands; to master server, who wore a lace-trimmed surplice. After every Mass, Fr. Gahan gathered the altar servers up for a quick review of the Mass or other liturgical events. He asked them, "Did anyone see anything?" and offered critiques. Altar serving under Fr. Gahan is where they learned reverence for the Mass and Jesus in the Eucharist—deep impressions they carry for the rest of their lives. What a tremendous gift!

A parishioner commented, "Then, there is 'The Voice' during Mass. Fr. Gahan's booming voice! Certainly the Marines gave him that. How can you not love listening to his voice during Mass? There is nothing like it. Inspirational, moving, loving, devoted . . . loud and clear."

Mass is now regularly offered in a beautiful traditional church made possible by the parishioners of St. Paul the Apostle parish, a dynamic priest, and most of all our Lord and the Blessed Mother.

Chapter Fifteen

Priesthood

"I call Fr. Gahan a breath of fresh air because we found him to be approachable on day one. He was one of us. There were no big I's and little yous. He made sure we knew how important we were. Considering the power the priesthood holds, he knew how to balance the field. Being a colonel in the Marine Corps was impressive as well. Let's just say he made us all better," a member of the parish staff commented.

Some of the parish staff's first impression of Fr. Gahan was intimidating, even "scared to death!" They saw a picture of him and he looked so solemn and formal, military all the way. However, the first day he came into the parish office, it was like he'd lived there all his life, and they all immediately began to relax. He became a part of the parish family. One staff member recalls, "When he saw my grandson, he always invited him into his office. I have a special picture of my grandson wearing Fr. Gahan's cap on his First Holy Communion day." The parishioners were impressed by his incredible memory. He remembered people by name and loved his parishioners. "His life experience made him special. The way he treated people, not just people he worked with or parishioners but people on the streets, there was a true sense of humility which formed his character," recalls a parishioner.

A parishioner recalled, "Looking back at the beautiful relationship we had with Fr. Gahan, I felt (selfishly) that God brought him to Spartanburg just for our family. Like the expression 'God never closes one door without opening another,' Fr. Gahan arrived when we needed him most. He drew us closer to God and in community with friends at church. I know from hearing countless Fr. Gahan stories over the years that many other people felt the same way. He was a breath of fresh air and a strong leader for our church. My husband and I had always attended Sunday Mass wherever we lived but Fr. Gahan is by far the most amazing priest we have ever known. I do not remember the first time we invited Fr. Gahan over to share a meal, but he has blessed our table many times. Whenever we invited friends over, we would include Fr. Gahan. He was the life of the party too, sharing hilarious stories that had everyone in stitches. He always took time to talk to the children and show them a trick or tell them a joke, or even shoot them with a Nerf gun as they ran in the backyard! A few expressions come to mind when I think of Fr. Gahan. Go big or go home, feel the love, and all in!"

At St. Paul the Apostle Church parish office, Fr. Gahan had a folding camp cot so that he could take a quick nap and stretch out the workday. He put in some really long hours in the parish. He also had a replica grenade on a board that read "Complaint Department, Take a Number." The tag with the number "1" on it was attached to the grenade pin. If you took the number, you would blow yourself up. This was sitting prominently on his desk. This was something that his parishioners were not expecting to see on a priest's desk!

Dr. Thomas Leong, one of his parishioners, recalled, "He would *always* be at daily Mass. Rain, shine, snow, or ice, Fr. Gahan would offer Mass. When others would try to convince him to stay home in ice storms, he would say, 'Well, someone might show up and would be disappointed if Mass had been canceled.' One time I saw him standing on a two-inch sheet of ice. He had a walking stick in his left hand and the other hand on someone's car. It was twenty minutes before Mass. He said, 'Thomas, how about a little help getting across this parking lot?' We shuffled across the ice and had Mass." Another parishioner recalled, "A frigid winter morning before 7:00 a.m., another parishioner and I waited in the yet to be warmed up historic church for confession. Fr. Gahan came in with a hot cup of coffee and offered us both a sip of hot java. We chitchatted a bit and then hit the confessional. How cool, sharing coffee with our confessor. What a wonderful way to begin the day. Not only does he pour himself out for us, he pours his coffee out for us, too!"

Fr. Gahan came to several rosary parties at parishioners' homes. He would always show up in his cassock. Often, he would sip a Guinness and socialize with everyone. People would line up to exchange words with him and share bits of their lives. His reverence made him deeply appreciated by those around him. But when the little kids would bring out their Nerf guns, he would grab a gun and start shooting all of them. He would yell, "I got you! I got you!" He had incredible joy while doing this! The kids would roll around in the grass with glee. Fr. Gahan could remember many details about everyone's children. These interactions contributed to encouraging young men from the parish to pursue the priesthood.

Fr. Gahan became good friends with Dr. Eric Rice, pastor of Trinity AME Zion Church of Whitmire, South Carolina. Dr. Rice recalled, "The first time he visited our church, my members asked me, 'Who is that man?' Fr. Gahan was dressed with a cassock, fascia, and shoulder cape. I replied, 'He will introduce himself shortly.' As the service began, I paused and asked him to greet the people. He stood up and introduced himself as a friend of the family and was delighted to participate in worship that morning with the assembly, and concluded by giving the congregation a blessing in Latin. They didn't understand the words of the blessing, but were impressed! After the worship service, Father didn't just leave. He mingled in fellowship with the parishioners. They began to ask about him week after week until he showed up again. We often pray for him, his entire family, and his health on a regular basis. We love our 'Father G.' He is probably the only Roman Catholic priest with an honorary membership in an African Methodist Episcopal Church. I could go on and on about him, he had such an impact on my life and the lives of my children. What can I say? I just love the man."

Fr. Gahan's life experience made him special to his parishioners. At the very first staff meeting held, he asked one of the staff, "I am going to need for you to do a special secret mission. My son and his family are coming for Christmas and we will need a babysitter for my grandchildren." So babysitters were lined up, a first for a priest!

Fr. Gahan made a military connection with a number of parishioners. One parishioner learned that Fr. Gahan was stationed in Thailand in 1972 at the same time he was stationed there. From then on, whenever they would see each other, they would use the Thai greeting, which includes a slight bow and upright hands pressed together as done while praying. Then they would add the word *Sawadi-krap*, meaning "hello," "good day," and even "goodbye."

Susan Leong recalled, "It was wonderful getting to know Fr. Gahan's family. His grandkids were close in age to our kids, and they hit it off right away. The first time I met his daughter Katie was when she and her family visited for Christmas. They came and picked up our kids and took them to Dollar General for shopping. Fr. Gahan let them each pick out a toy for each of their parents and siblings, but not for themselves. Then they took them over to the rectory and wrapped them up. They had so much fun and could barely contain their excitement for us to open the special gifts they picked out. Once more they experienced the joy of giving. Fr. Gahan encouraged us to visit Terence and Kate on a planned trip to Texas. Although we were going to see old friends in Corpus Christi, the highlight was staying at the Gahan home in Lockhart, Texas! We have remained good friends ever since."

The parish had a grammar school, which Fr. Gahan especially enjoyed visiting frequently. He gave out the report card to each student. Reports were electronic, so each student would look at the screen with him, reviewing grades, especially the grade for effort. He made sure that there was a strong Catholic character maintained in the school. Catholicism was reinforced in everything they did throughout the day. If Fr. Gahan ever got exasperated and nothing seemed to be going right at his office, he would take a quick walk to the school to see the children for a needed boost. Every Friday during the school year Fr. Gahan offered a school

Mass. At the close of Mass, he would ask students grade appropriate questions about the homily or readings for that day. As an example, asking the younger students, "Does God love you?" Or the older students where a saint of the day was from, and where the country was located. For correct answers, he would give the students a brand-new, crisp $2 bill, JFK half dollar, or gold Sacagawea dollar. The students loved it, and it certainly encouraged alertness and attention at Mass. Over time, Fr. Gahan noticed that the students knew the readings and saint of the day very well. He discovered that teachers would review the readings and saints the day before Mass so the children were raring to go with the knowledge, and eager for a chance to earn a prize!

Fr. Gahan with students of St. Paul the Apostle Parish School on All Saints' Day. At right, enjoying his parishioners, Fr. Gahan relaxing at a St. Paul the Apostle parish social event.

Fr. Gahan loves sports, especially the University of Notre Dame football. One day he went to watch the St. Joseph Catholic High School soccer team play in Greenville. When he arrived, the game was already at halftime, and the St. Joseph team was losing and discouraged. When the play restarted, Fr. Gahan brought out "The Voice" on the sidelines, and cheered the team to victory!

St. Paul the Apostle parishioners have expressed their inspiration by being close to someone who is selfless, generous, and a hard worker. They appreciated all that Fr. Gahan did for their church. He could have been relaxing and enjoying his retirement years, but they were so glad that he said "yes" to God when called to the priesthood. Despite the long hours and difficult tasks, he was cheerful, humble, and took time to build relationships. With his magnanimous personality he could connect with people from all walks of life, and people loved him!

Fr. Gahan became close to many of the parishioners. Dr. Leong recalled, "I remember going to lunch one day with Fr. Gahan and my wife, Susan. She was well into the pregnancy with our fourth child. We so loved Fr. Gahan that we told him that if we had a son, we would name him Timothy after Fr. Gahan." Susan Leong stated, "One of my all-time best memories was an idea that Fr. Gahan had. To celebrate our Timothy's first birthday, Fr. Gahan suggested celebrating with all the young families in our parish. He wanted to host a huge party! He remembered when stationed in Hawaii how first birthdays were celebrated with a special luau where everyone was invited. He had many of our closest friends working on this party. Everyone helped in a special way. Some brought food, including a pig slow-roasted Hawaiian style with an apple in its mouth! One of the more artistic parishioners made a beautiful banner with a Hawaiian *aloha* birthday message. It was an amazing and unforgettable party with a big group of church friends, delicious food, a magician, a bouncy house and toys for all the kids, face painting, fishing, petting zoo, and teenagers playing DJ! The kids still talk about that unforgettable party. It was also one of the many times Fr. Gahan voiced his desire to make a grand entrance by parachute!"

Fr. Timothy M. Gahan at first birthday party of Timothy M. Leong, September 2012, Spartanburg, South Carolina

One summer, Fr. Gahan had a roommate, Fr. Michel Bineen-Mukad from the Democratic Republic of Congo. He was a transitional deacon living at the rectory while assigned to a chaplaincy program at the Spartanburg Regional Medical Center. Fr. Michel ended up being a fantastic roommate, friend, and priest. But he had to survive Fr. Gahan's friendly hazing, which involved questioning about which dangerous animals Fr. Michel had personally killed with a spear, etc.

Once Fr. Michel was cooking some exotic soup at the rectory and had to leave. He accidently left the house with the stove top on. A while later, the house was full of smoke, and the fire department showed up. They broke in and turned off the burner. They called Fr. Gahan to come air out the house. Fortunately, nothing was really damaged. Fr. Michel showed up in all of the commotion and didn't realize that he had left the stove top on. Trying to make light of the situation, Fr. Gahan asked him, "Hey, Michel, I thought we were friends. Why are you trying to burn down our house?" Fr. Michel successfully completed the program and was ordained not long thereafter, and they became the best of friends.

Fr. Gahan allowed an Emmaus Retreat ministry to sprout and flourish in the parish. Emmaus is a Catholic retreat program open to people of all Christian communities. It provided the opportunity to reconnect with what matters and share faith journeys. Since 2011, over 800 people have attended these retreats in small groups. Fr. Gahan has been to almost every Emmaus Retreat, twenty-three of them, even after retirement. He continues to drive six hours roundtrip to the retreat center three times per year to support the Emmaus evangelization. Hundreds are grateful for his love and support through Emmaus. He won't admit it because he's a Marine, but he loves the *abrazos*!

Fr. Gahan's devotion to the Blessed Mother had a real impact on the parish community. A parishioner states, "Many who seldom ever prayed the rosary are saying rosaries every day now. To Jesus through Mary. Thank you, Fr. Gahan, for showing us your love for Mary, Our Mother, through planting miraculous medals throughout the church during construction of our new church, and the installation of brown scapulars!"

Fr. Timothy M. Gahan received the Fr. John J. Monahan Leadership Award, October 2014. The award is presented annually by the Society of St. Paul the Apostle. At right, Fr. Gahan baptizing his grandson Conan Mannix Gahan, October 2008.

Fred Ricardi and his wife, Sharon, recall, "In January of 2015, we approached Father to inquire about having a Divine Mercy Holy Hour the first Sunday after Easter. The previous year some parishioners gathered to pray the Divine Mercy Chaplet, but there was no associated Holy Hour. We met with Father and discussed a proposed Divine Mercy program pamphlet that Sharon had compiled. Fr. Gahan saw our enthusiasm, and was kind, not wanting us to be disappointed with the turnout and response he expected. He said it would be great if we had fifty in attendance. Fr. Gahan celebrated a magnificent, heartfelt, and soul-searching Divine Mercy Holy Hour! Although not in the program or schedule, after the Holy Hour attendees started lining up at the confessional. Father was there for more than an additional hour. With more than 200 people in attendance, Father indicated he was thankful and grateful for the response and especially the confessions. This Divine Mercy Holy Hour continued after Father left as one of his legacies."

In May 2015, the last year Fr. Gahan was at Spartanburg, the parish held a surprise seventieth birthday party for him. It happened to fall on the Feast of Pentecost. In the parish there was a tradition of holding a Pentecost potluck celebrating the feast, so the parishioners decided to roll it into a surprise party for Fr. Gahan. As a parishioner recalled, "He typically doesn't like to call attention to himself, and did not want a birthday celebration. He is a very special man, not just as a priest or pastor, but as a very good friend. We wanted to make his birthday a big deal. Prior to the Saturday night Mass, Fr. Gahan was shocked to see his son Terence and daughter Katie standing in the narthex. The parishioners couldn't believe that they were able to keep it all a surprise! There was a picture display, a cake with a Marine Corps emblem on it, and the gym was packed. Everyone wanted to be a part of it. It is a birthday party everyone will never forget!"

Our family has had the honor of having our brother attend special events in our lives. He offered the fiftieth wedding anniversary Mass for my sister Sheila and our brother-in-law Joe. The reception after the Mass was fun, with eight siblings together, just as we had been fifty years earlier. Our cousin Bonnie and her husband Bill also celebrated their fiftieth wedding anniversary with

Fr. E. Corbett Walsh, SJ, Bonnie's brother, offering the anniversary Mass with Fr. Gahan as concelebrant. Years later, when Fr. Walsh died unexpectedly, Fr. Gahan concelebrated the funeral Mass with the New England Province Jesuit Community.

Fr. E. Corbett Walsh, SJ, offering Mass with his cousin Fr. Gahan on the occasion of his sister Bonnie and Bill Stoloski's fiftieth wedding anniversary, July 2010. At right, the three amigos: my brothers Ted, Tim, and Michael attending my sister Sheila's fiftieth wedding anniversary reception, May 2012.

In August 2015, Fr. Gahan retired from active ministry and moved back to Columbia. Since his retirement, he substitutes periodically at local parishes. He helps with retreats and offers Mass and administers sacraments at different parishes in the Midlands region of South Carolina when requested. He has a small chapel in his home in which he offers daily Mass.

Parishioner Jody Armstrong remembered, "My wife, Mary, told me one day it has been amazing how many women have said to her since Fr. Gahan left our parish, 'Who am I going to talk to now that Fr. Gahan is gone?' Mary wondered to herself if he has the ability to bilocate! One day, early in 2020, while our son was home from a break during his mission year, I asked him, 'Andrew, who has had the most impact on your faith life?' 'Fr. Gahan' was his answer almost before I could finish the question. 'And serving on the altar with him.'"

His home in Columbia has a sign in Irish over the fireplace. The Irish reads "There is no fireplace like your own fireplace." He takes "Rosary walks" most days, and has a set of the Stations of the Cross in his backyard. Fr. Gahan has experienced health issues. Four months after retiring, he had a heart attack, later came total reverse shoulder replacement, total knee replacement, and open-heart surgery.

A young man, a student at the University of South Carolina, remembers Fr. Gahan filling in for the pastor of a church in downtown Columbia. "I wasn't familiar with the priest who was offering Mass that day. He seemed a bit 'old school.' After Mass, I asked if he could hear my confession. He did and he was great, so friendly and funny. Later, my twin brother and I went to a Pro Life banquet and auction. Fr. Gahan was there and didn't know I had a twin, so we surprised him." The twin brothers attended Mass daily at different Catholic churches; however, Fr. Gahan had never seen them together. From then on, when Fr. Gahan needed help at home, the twin brothers were always ready and willing to help. "What I have learned most from Fr. Gahan is to follow God's will, which was so reassuring to hear, like a breath of fresh air. Having been a married person and then priest, Fr. Gahan is certainly understanding." The young man stated, "Some of the most spiritually moving Masses have been private Masses at his home. When Fr. Gahan offers Mass, he is reverent and serious. Each movement is planned and powerful." The student is currently in medical school, and his twin brother is a seminarian studying for the priesthood for the Diocese of Charleston.

In late spring 2018, James Gannone, author of *The Rest Is Small Potatoes*, and his wife, Chris, visited my brother in Columbia. Jim was aboard the troop transport ship USNS *Simon B. Buckner* in September 1966 with then Private First Class Gahan sailing to Vietnam. My brother hosted a dinner party for the Gannones at which the twin brothers tended the bar and served the dinner. One of the brothers stated, "It was amazing to watch Fr. Gahan as a host, always keeping conversation going, and meeting the needs of all in attendance. We learned so much from him just by example."

In 2017 our brother Ted was diagnosed with lung cancer. In April of the following year, the Gahan clan gathered in Ohio to visit with him and his family. The siblings enjoyed being together and sharing memories. A Mass was offered for Ted in his home, surrounded by family, by his brother. During the Mass, Tim administered the Sacrament of the Sick to his "Irish twin" brother whose life was so intertwined with his. What blessings flowed that day. Our beloved brother Theodore Patrick Gahan Jr. passed away one month later. His wife Sandy, children, and grandchildren were nearby.

Fr. Gahan administering the Sacrament of the Sick to our brother Ted with his wife, Sandy, by his side, April 2018. Ted died one month later.

My brother's best friend in Columbia is Tom Burbage, a retired businessman and retired Air Force officer. He and Tim have a special relationship. He calls Tim "Colonel Padre." Burbage recalled, "I was raised Methodist. However, I went to Mass with my wife and children, who were Catholic. I got to know him well at Myrtle Beach. After Mass, Fr. Gahan would join us for breakfast. He started giving me instructions in the Catholic faith over pancakes, eggs, and sausage. As time passed, I reached a point where he brought me into the faith. I am so happy that I am Catholic. I have learned so much. I was received into the Catholic faith in the beautiful historic St. Paul the Apostle Church in Spartanburg with my wife, Mary Jo, and two daughters present. It was just us. It was so personal. This was a major event in my life."

Time with family has always been important to my brother. Every Thanksgiving the family gets together at his daughter's home in Kansas, and every Christmas at his son's home in Texas. During the summer he and his children and grandchildren spend time together at the beach.

Gahan family together for Thanksgiving 2015.

Some may ask, "How is it that a career Marine officer becomes a priest?" Many think of Marines as the stern drill instructor and moving portrayals of "John Wayne type" individuals. How is it that they have a spiritual side? Lt. Bob Simi, a young combat engineer platoon commander who served with Lieutenant Colonel Gahan during a deployment to the Mediterranean Sea, Southern Europe, and the Middle East in 1991, answered these questions this way: "There are similarities between Catholics and Marines. What are the similarities? It took me years and life experience to answer that question. When I look back at my life and other Catholic Marine friends like Fr. Gahan, I think the answer comes down to love. Different people have definitions of love, but that was what probably attracted me to the Marine Corps originally. That is what made the commanding officer and others like him so incredibly impactful. It is the deep love they have for their subordinates. Love can take different forms. Sometimes it is called for when disciplining another—what we call in the church 'spiritual works of mercy' to admonish the sinner."

He continued, "All Marines have an instant bond, especially among the civilian population. If they are Catholic and a Marine, then you go deep pretty quickly. Back to why. In my personal experience, the values are very much in alignment, particularly in leadership. It comes down to the concept of self-sacrifice and putting others before yourself. I was attracted to the Marines knowing it was going to be demanding, not only physically but mentally and morally. Leaders attempt to constantly be an example and put Marines before yourself. There is a huge level of comfort that moment that you realize that your commanding officer is a devout Catholic. In life-and-death situations you ask yourself who do I really trust on a super deep level when you need it? Who answers to a much higher call? He has to be able to trust his subordinates with major responsibilities to close the loop. To know that your commanding officer has that deep faith was a huge level of comfort for me. The average civilian would not think of a Marine for humility. Having a deep level of humility probably made Fr. Gahan a successful Marine Corps officer. Humility in leadership is not contradictory; it is more than complementary, it is parallel. Embracing the Catholic faith makes one a better Marine Corps leader. As St. Paul said, 'It is no longer I who live, but Christ lives in me.' The more you become Christlike, the better leader you are."

Throughout his life as a son, brother, husband, father, Marine, and Roman Catholic priest, Tim has strived to know and do God's will. In writing his philosophy, my brother quoted John Henry Cardinal Newman, "God has created me to do Him some definite service; He has committed some work to me, which He has not committed to another . . ." My brother wrote "Cardinal Newman was right—we were created to do God some definite service. The challenge for each of us is first to discover our particular mission, and then to complete it with faithfulness." God committed multiple works to Fr. Gahan and the grace to faithfully carry out those missions to successful completion. May his remaining days be long, healthy, and happy, and the Blessed Mother and St. Joseph be his constant companion.

About The Author

Colleen McFall, grew up in a military family, one of nine children, in which duty to God, family and country were cornerstones of family life. She has seen her older brother, Tim, live an interesting and challenging life of service to all three. As a high school sophomore Colleen remembers praying for her brother while he served in the Marine Corps as a helicopter machine gunner in Vietnam, and during the many years thereafter when he was deployed elsewhere in Asia, to the Mediterranean Sea and the Middle East. She has been witness to the role faith has played in his life as a Marine, husband, father and Roman Catholic priest.

Colleen is a Registered Nurse and enjoys living on a small spread in East Texas with her husband, Terry, especially when their five children and 13 grandchildren visit.

CPSIA information can be obtained
at www.ICGtesting.com
Printed in the USA
JSHW040812120322
23655JS00002B/12